Behind the Fireplace

~Memories of a girl working in the Dutch Wartime Resistance~

Recounted by Grietje Scott

Written by Andrew Scott

Copyright © 1992, 2016 by Andrew Scott & Grietje Scott

Published by the author using CreateSpace.com

All Rights Reserved

No part of this publication may be reproduced, distributed, or transmitted in any form or by any means, including photocopying, recording, or other electronic or mechanical methods, without the prior written permission of the author, except in the case of brief quotations embodied in critical reviews and certain other non-commercial uses permitted by copyright law.

For permission requests, write to:

Andrew Scott: BehindTheFireplace@gmail.com

While every effort has been made to afford sensitivity to the people and events as recounted in this biography, the author and/or publisher shall have neither liability nor responsibility to anyone with respect to any loss or damage caused, or alleged to be caused, directly or indirectly, by the information contained in this book.

Book design by *Andrew Scott*
Cover design by *Andrew Scott*
Cover photograph © *Andrew Scott and Grietje Scott*
Editing by *Nicky Beele Editing, UK*

ISBN: 1523356995
ISBN-13: 978-1523356997

Contents

Preface 4
    Map of Holland 10
Part 1 12
Part 2 208
Epilogue: 2012 – A 90th Birthday Party 275
Acknowledgements 278
Annex 1: Chronology of Events 281
    Part 1 281
    Part 2 283
Annex 2: A Letter from Kees 285
Annex 3: Comments on the Books by the Refugees' Families 288
Annex 4: A Poem by Salomon (Piet) 292

Preface

One day, as a child in Scotland in the early 1960s, my teacher at junior school asked us to find out what our parents had done during the Second World War. My mother talked of her life in Holland and used the words 'Jews behind the fireplace', but when she tried to explain further, she became so emotional that she was unable to say more. I eventually reported back to my teacher on my father's work in an anti-aircraft battery, but I sensed there was an untold story that I did not yet understand.

It was to be almost forty years before I was to discover the extraordinary narrative behind these words, and another twenty before the story was talked of outside the family. It is with a sense of respect and pride that I now share this story with you, as testimony to my mother's courage and determination in the face of the deeply traumatic events the war unleashed in her world.

My mother's story is a profound story of two distinct parts. During World War II, she and her family, the Okmas, sheltered seven people hiding from the Gestapo, six of them Jews, and this led to her becoming absorbed into the Dutch Resistance as part of a team fighting the Nazis. After the war, the second part of her ordeal began.

She had initially joined the Resistance as a payback for the support her family was receiving in sheltering the Jews. At first her role had been minor, but as the war progressed, the dangers increased, and by the end she had escaped the clutches of the Gestapo four times, the last occasion being when she alone, out of a group of some twenty Dutch folk, escaped a firing squad. The events left their legacy, and for years she would wake up at screaming point, overwhelmed by the image of a German soldier silhouetted against a grey sky, pointing his rifle at her as she cowered on the ground.

In 1962, she had eventually sought help from a psychiatrist for her debilitating distress. His diagnosis threatened the very fabric of her family. For eighteen years she lived with his threat looming over her until the last of her children left home. It was only in the 1970s and 1980s – when other organisations started to formally recognise her role in the war – that this recognition gave her the confidence to finally talk to the family about the events of that time.

In 1979, she and her family received recognition with the award of the *Medal of the Righteous*, from the Israeli organisation *Yad Vashem*. In 1980, she applied for a pension from the Dutch Foundation, *Stichting 1940-1945*, an organisation funded to help former members of the wartime Resistance. As she prepared for a hearing, she needed to find a witness to provide independent testimony to the Foundation. Her boyfriend during the war had been a commander in the Resistance and he agreed to provide testimony. The letter from this recognised Resistance commander had concluded with the words '...if you could capture in words what she did when she was in the Resistance, you would capture the essence of what the Resistance was all about.'

The writing of this story started in 1992, when I was stationed in Washington DC. My mother had come to visit me for two weeks, and on the first evening, the conversation had drifted back to the Second World War. She had started talking, first about one event, then another, painting vivid vignettes of times past. She is not a natural storyteller, and I quickly became confused as she hopped back and forth in time, leaving many tales part-told, or trailing randomly into other unrelated events. Over some five years I stitched together the fragments, reviewed it with family members and refined it until it held together. It was circulated round the family, and the recounting and writing gave my mother a degree of therapy and helped put the more strident memories to rest. In 2012, as we celebrated her 90th birthday, we told the local paper a bit about what had happened. The story rapidly gained the attention of the Scottish press, and strangers in the sheltered home where she lived started approaching her and congratulating her, something that gave her a quiet pleasure.

Over the years, I was able to trace descendants of all the Jews who had hidden in the house and, through their comments, gain insight into their parents' experiences, which I have incorporated in this book. The appearance in the press also helped others trace my mother. In 2015, seventy years after the end of the war, the descendants of her wartime boyfriend were able to locate the article in the Scottish press and use it to track her down, and we were able to exchange memories of these past events. Some final pieces of the puzzle fell into place.

This is my mother's story. It is the story of a young, single woman in Occupied Holland. She was christened Grietje[1], but was affectionately called Kieks by everyone.

The events described here occurred fifty years before I first started to write them down. The first strands my mother related with intensity and anger: anger directed towards the Germans, the Jews, her family, everyone, and most especially psychiatrists. With the retelling, her anger subsided and in some cases was redirected. This is not a contemporaneous account, but an attempt to unscramble confused memories, many of which had been locked away unspoken for half a century. There may inevitably be mistakes, inconsistencies and ambiguities, but I believe these do not detract from the essence of the overall story. All the major events that shaped her war have been included in the story.

Finally, I recognise that the experiences she and her family went through were not unique in Holland. When the war ended, thousands of Jewish refugees appeared on the streets all around the country. The people of Holland hid many Jews during the war; these Jews were sheltered

---

[1] Pronunciation: Grietje = H*ree*-chuh (G is a guttural h); Kieks = Keeks.

by individuals and families such as the Okmas, and these other families suffered similar experiences and pressures. This book is dedicated to all these families.

Grietje Okma Scott died in her sleep on 4th January 2016.

Kieks on her 90th birthday

Map of Holland

Leeuwarden	– the Okma family's hometown from 1922 - 1936
Utrecht	– the family's hometown from 1936 - 1939
The Hague	– Holland's administrative capital; the family's home town during the war
Arnhem	– Ruurd's home for most of the war
Haarlem	– **Hillegom**, where Douwe lived, is just south of Haarlem.

Haarlemmermeer (Haarlem's Lake), is just west of Haarlem is where Kees operated

Dordrecht – the town where Kees went after he left Citroenstraat.

Willemsdorp is just south of Dordrecht, on the bank of the river

Coevorden – the town where the Hekschers lived before the war

Groningen – the town where Trijntje lived for a few months after getting married

Twello – the town where Ruurd was staying when Kieks visited him in January 1945

Part 1

There is a famous Chinese curse: 'May you live in interesting times.' Some people wonder why this is called a curse. There are other people whose children repeatedly ask to be told stories of times gone by, stories they themselves only want to forget. These people understand the curse of 'living in interesting times'. In the aftermath of World War I, Adolf Hitler was starting his rise to power and would spread the shadow of this curse over all of Europe, but in the Holland of 1922, this shadow was faint and far away. With an economic boom under way, universal suffrage finally becoming a reality, life was good in the most pleasant of ways – and for historians perhaps even a little bit dull.

In January that year, Kieks was born in the small town of Leeuwarden in Friesland, a rural province in the north of Holland. For some it is perhaps an interesting part of the country. A region with its own culture, dialect and ancient language, in Holland it is known for its beautiful lakes and the exceptional height of its inhabitants. Kieks' father was Dirk Okma, a lawyer and district court judge who had lived in Leeuwarden for over twenty years, where he had met and married Truida, whom the family called *'Moeder'*[2], with Kieks the youngest of their eight children. The eldest was Martha, who was 15 years old when Kieks was born, and who had been followed in regular succession by three boys: Ruurd 14, Willem 12, and Douwe 10. They in turn were followed by three girls: Trijntje 8, Ella 5, and Moeder's namesake, Truida, who was 3 at Kieks' birth.

Kieks had been christened Grietje, but when she first went to school there were no fewer than eight girls in her class with the same name. Each had their own nickname, and everyone, including the teacher, used the pet name she had been given by her family: Kieks.

Their peaceful life held no foreshadow of the 'interesting times' that would later befall Kieks and her family. They lived comfortably in the small town, enjoying frequent camping holidays and sailing trips on a lake some miles distant. Life was very pleasant.

---

[2] Pronunciation: Moeder = _Mooder_; Martha = _Mar-tuh_; Ruurd = _Rürt_; Willem = _Villum_; Douwe = _Daw-vuh_; Trijntje = _Train-chuh_; Truida = _Trow-duh_ (Trow rhyming with 'brow').

The Okma family, circa 1928
From left,
back: Douwe, Martha, Ruurd, Trijntje, Truida, Willem;
front: Father, Kieks, Ella, Moeder (Mother)

In September 1929, when Kieks was 7, Father contracted an infection while sitting in court, and died suddenly after a very short illness. The family was devastated. There was little money to cover the needs of his family after he died, and the events left his widow distraught and unable to cope. With the world in the grip of the Great Depression, money now very tight and with a family to support, in

1936 Moeder sold the house and moved to a rented home in Utrecht. By this time, Kieks' older siblings were starting to leave home, with her eldest brother, Ruurd, moving away in 1936 to live in Arnhem with his new bride, a girl called Corrie Vos[3].

Kieks in Utrecht, circa 1937

By the mid 1930s, Kieks' older siblings Willem and Martha were occasionally travelling together on summer vacations. In the summer of 1938 they had travelled together down the Rhineland in Germany on a canoeing holiday, but had become uncomfortably aware of the pernicious state-organised anti-Semitism they saw around them, and had been shocked by the indifference of

---

[3] Pronunciation: Vos = *Fohss*.

passers-by when Jews were being harassed in the street. The dark throes of Nazi anti-semitism and persecution were gathering momentum.

Just a few months after the holiday, the Okma family were to see newsreels of the horrors of *Kristallnacht*, when on the 9th and 10th November 1938, Nazi supporters swarmed the streets of many towns in Germany, smashing the windows of synagogues and Jewish-owned shops, strewing the streets with shards of glass that glistened like fragments of crystal in the moonlight. They saw images of several of the towns that Willem and Martha had visited earlier, images that moved them deeply; images that would influence Willem's thinking when the war finally started.

Disgusted by the events they had witnessed, Willem and Martha couldn't face the prospect of returning to Germany for their next vacation in the early summer of 1939, and instead decided to travel over to Glasgow. The city had received a lot of publicity in the papers in 1938 because of the Empire Exhibition, a large spectacle and exposition celebrating Britain's Empire and Scotland's role in it. They had a good time, and for a little while put aside thoughts of the clouds gathering over Europe, as they explored the city and enjoyed features described in the reports of the Exhibition.

Afterwards, journeying by train to the city of Hull to catch the ferry on to Rotterdam, they met a Scotsman, Archie Scott, setting out on his first trip to the continent. Willem and Martha could hardly speak a word of English, while Archie couldn't speak any Dutch. However, they had each learnt a little French at school, and Archie had perhaps more confidence in his French than his skills justified. So, with a combination of pidgin French and plenty of gesticulations, they passed the time genially to Hull. Once they arrived, Archie said farewell and disappeared to collect his bag from the guard van.

A few minutes later they came across him again on the platform. His luggage had just been sent on the wrong train down to London. The railways had promised to bring it back in a couple of days, but Archie announced that he would travel on without it. He had only two weeks' holiday a year and did not want to spend half of it waiting for a suitcase.

Willem invited him to visit the family at Utrecht, so Archie travelled with them and spent a week with the Okmas until his luggage finally arrived. In Utrecht he met the other family members, including Kieks who was now 17, and provided entertainment for all as he continued to communicate with them using mime and his unique pidgin French. Kieks was amused at just how bad his French was, but she was impressed at his willingness to make the effort to communicate, and at his remaining unfazed when his attempts raised the occasional laugh.

Soon after coming to Utrecht, Willem accepted a job offer in a meat-processing company, a job that meant he had to move to The Hague. At about the same time, his other brother, Douwe, announced he was going to get married, so the family was again in flux.

As 1939 rolled on, Willem went house hunting and eventually found a suitable apartment for the family. The address was 18 Citroenstraat[4], located in an anonymous middle-class street in a maze of similar ones in the suburbs of The Hague. The building was attached to the end of a row of three-storey houses that had been constructed a few years earlier, and formed a continuous terrace with another apartment block on the other side, abutting onto the building's stairwell. Their apartment was quite

---

[4] Pronunciation: Citroenstraat = *Sitroonstraht*.

generous in size, taking up the top three of four floors, with two reception rooms on the lowest floor, and three bedrooms on the floor above. On the top floor there was another bedroom and a small boxroom, which Willem agreed to convert into a workroom. At the back, there were small open-air walkways on the second and third floors that were just wide enough to hang out washing to dry.

Citroenstraat 18, in The Hague. The nearest building (garage plus two ground-floor windows) is the neighbour's house. Number 18 is located between this house and the line of identical houses, and includes all except the ground floor (See also later photos)

A family portrait shortly before the war; back row: Ruurd, Moeder; front row: Truida, Kieks, Ella

Willem was pleased with the apartment and invited the rest of the family in Utrecht to join him in The

Hague. Kieks had found it difficult to settle in Utrecht, and so in some ways was quite happy with the move, although a little disappointed that the new apartment was smaller than the one in Utrecht, and that she would now have to share a bedroom with her eldest sister, Martha. Her brother, Douwe, would not be joining them, as he was now engaged to be married, and she was very conscious that the family was dispersing, as her siblings began to meet partners and go their separate ways. She was not ready to do that yet, but she wondered how many of the others would soon be making new lives for themselves and moving on. Perhaps there would be more space for her in the house before long.

In May, as international tensions grew and war threatened, most of the Okmas moved into the house. Douwe stayed behind in Utrecht until two months later when he got married and, with his bride Tiny[5], left for a house in Hillegom, a pretty village in the tulip fields some forty kilometres to the north, just south of Haarlem. With the new arrangements, the four-bedroom house was to be shared by the seven of them: Moeder, Martha (who was now 32), Willem, Ella, Trijntje, Truida and Kieks (now 17).

---

[5] Pronunciation: Tiny = *Tee-nee*; Hillegom = <u>Hill</u>-*uh*-<u>h</u>*om* (*g* is a guttural *h*).

Douwe and Tiny marry in August 1939

Kieks just before the war

Kieks had just failed her school-leaving exams in Utrecht, so as soon as the move was completed she registered locally for evening classes to re-sit them, and also signed up for a professional needlework class.

Settling in, Kieks increasingly enjoyed the new location. There were now quite a few other family members nearby; aunts and cousins whom she had only seen infrequently before. One was Kieks' cousin, Guido van Deth, who lived in a suburb of Amsterdam. Guido was a couple of years older than Kieks, and they became good friends soon after the move from Utrecht, meeting up frequently and enjoying each other's company. He was a puppeteer, making a living from a marionette show, and by 1938, had an assistant whom he had recruited a year or two previously. She was of Dutch East Indies origin, and he had selected her because of her good looks and her jet-black complexion. He was convinced her dramatic looks would surely distinguish his act from any others, which seemed to work, because he had occasional bookings at the Royal Palace where he entertained Queen Wilhelmina's children.

In September 1939, just a few months after the family had moved to The Hague, war broke out between Britain and Germany. Though Germany had issued a guarantee of neutrality to Holland, Martial Law was nevertheless declared that month and, as the Dutch troops were gradually mobilised, Willem was drafted.

The family was not too worried; they could not believe that Holland would really fight their German neighbours, and in any case, they were a religious family who devoutly believed in God and they were convinced that He would look after Willem.

He was posted to the German border from where the invasion would surely come. Despite the policy of neutrality, the Germans invaded Holland on the 10th May 1940 without a formal declaration of war. Within days they had bombed the centre of Rotterdam until it was little more than a shell. The 'Rotterdam Blitz', aimed mainly at civilian targets, destroyed 25,000 homes and killed around 900 civilians. Germany then gave an ultimatum that unless the country surrendered, another five cities would suffer the same fate. Holland surrendered, and by the end of May 1940 the country was occupied. The Dutch troops were ordered back to the barracks and confined under armed guard.

Willem in uniform after being drafted in 1940

The city of Rotterdam after being bombed by the Germans in May 1940

A few days after the surrender, Kieks decided to go to the local barracks and view the bomb damage that some of her friends had been talking about. She had been shocked at the sudden news of dramatic bombings and battles, and felt she needed to see with her own eyes some evidence of what was happening. She saw people milling about in the barracks grounds and found herself observing some rehearsal in the parade ground. The occupying forces seemed to be preparing for an event in the city centre, while a large number of Dutch soldiers stood lined against the perimeter fence, watching proceedings. Kieks spotted one soldier with his arm out behind him, waving a small card through the railings, hidden from the sight of the German guards. Curious, she went over and realised it was a postcard to his family. It reminded her of her own brother, and how the whole family was waiting anxiously for news.

So she took it and posted it in the nearby post box. When she looked round, there were now a few more cards being waved through the railings, and as she started collecting these, yet more appeared. She made a number of trips, realising that the soldiers were circulating to allow others to pass her their cards. Eventually the flow of cards dried up and Kieks went back home, pleased to have helped this subterfuge.

Left: A portrait of Kieks; right: the photograph from her ID papers at the start of the war. Her hair had to be wetted down to ensure the ear could be seen

A cousin of Kieks, Tine van Deth[6], was a police inspector who frequently called round to visit Martha. Kieks found her to be an intimidating woman and so tried to fade into the background whenever she visited. A few days after the postcard incident, Tine called round on one of her visits, and spotted Kieks in the living room,

---

[6] Pronunciation: Tine van Deth = *Tee-nuh fun Dett*.

discreetly attempting to leave. She challenged Kieks to explain what she was doing to resist the Occupation. When Kieks made no reply, Tine frowned. Couldn't she do more? Why, Tine had heard that even 'one of those tarts' from around the barracks had done her bit! The girl had gone round and collected a large pile of postcards from the soldiers and posted them. If the likes of 'that tart' could do something, surely Kieks could think of something useful? Kieks always found it difficult to talk to Tine, and was especially flustered this time, but was determined not to be associated with 'those tarts', and said nothing as she slipped out of the room.

Police Inspector Tine was in her late-forties. Soon after the invasion, she had started to organise a Resistance movement, gathering support from a large number of the police staff who worked with her. She worked on the principle that, by appearing to cooperate with the Germans, the Dutch police would be trusted more, which would give them more opportunities to spot and exploit German weaknesses. She was unable to carry out this role for long. She was arrested by the German occupying forces following an incident at an internment camp, and sent off to one of the special punishment camps that were being set up. Her offence had occurred at the time when the Dutch had been interning German citizens, just before the invasion. She had reprimanded a German woman who had tried to grab a towel during the registration process. When the occupying forces took over, the woman sought Tine out and had her arrested for 'insulting the German people'.

Willem returned home within a couple of months of the Occupation, but said little about his experiences at the front. The scenes in the newsreels of *Kristallnacht* preyed on his mind, and he feared how events might unfold in Holland.

Kieks was twelve years younger than the 30-year-old Willem, and as his little *zusje*[7], not particularly close. She sensed that something troubling was on his mind, and that he would not be discussing it with her.

A few days after he got home, the doorbell rang. When he answered the door, there before him were two postal workers making a special delivery. He was presented with a letter from overseas that had somehow

---

[7] Pronunciation: zusje = <u>zoo</u>-*shyuh*. Dutch: term of endearment for 'little sister'.

been allowed through, in spite of the war. On looking at it he realised that it was from Archie Scott, the man who had stayed with them the previous year. The letter had been forwarded via their old address in Utrecht, and simply thanked them for their hospitality and asked after their health. Willem took it from the senior officer, who clearly seemed to know the contents, and tried to casually explain how amusing it all was and how little contact they had had with the man. When he went back into the house, the family could see that he was unsettled by the event. He was very conscious of the web being cast by the new German Secret State Police, the *Gestapo*, and he sensed they would be watching how he responded. The letter was of no importance, but would the Gestapo realise that? Would the family now be under suspicion for having links with Britain?

Kieks' reaction to the letter was to think back to the happier times before the war and the relaxed atmosphere which seemed so far away. The letter had a deeper impact on Willem and seemed to galvanize him. He told the family he was not prepared to sit back and do nothing, and he started analysing the shape of the house, to see if there were any corners that might provide a good hiding space in the future.

There was a roof space above their apartment, but it would be the first place anyone would look in a search. However, there seemed to be a mismatch between the inside and the outside construct of the building, which he tried to resolve. He studied the house from every angle, and even climbed out onto the roof to get a different perspective. As he climbed through the skylight window, Kieks teased him, asking if she now had a squirrel for a brother.

However, as he clambered over the roof, Willem became increasingly excited. The roof ran to a large chimney stack, which incorporated the chimneys of their own house, before continuing to the neighbour's stairwell. When he looked closely, he became convinced that the structure was an architectural decoration, designed to cover the join between the two buildings, and was largely ornamental, probably containing a void. It adjoined their top floor, so if he could go through the wall of the boxroom, he would be able to get directly into that space.

Willem finally decided to put his hunch to the test. Grasping a hammer and chisel, he started knocking through the wall in the boxroom. With clouds of dust and debris billowing in all directions, he was soon able to make a small hole in the wall. Peeking through with a torch, he discovered a chamber some twenty-one feet long by about four feet wide (6.5m x 1.1m). The roof was only about four feet (1.2 metres) above floor level and would be too low for someone to stand upright under it, but there was plenty of space to store things. Excited about his discovery, Willem decided to convert it into a useable storage chamber. Kieks was amused at his animated reaction, but she was not convinced that the storage space was needed. However, she could tell that Willem was unsettled and had an urge to do something, and she felt that this was perhaps something harmless that would take his mind off the war and the oppressive atmosphere around them.

18 Citroenstraat, showing the structure where the secret room was located on the left (see arrow).

Detail showing the location of the hidden chamber on the skyline, to left of sloping roof (see arrow)

The common entrance stairwell for number 18 and other houses

Before he could set about converting the secret chamber, he felt he had to speak with his neighbour in the adjoining apartment, since the man was technically the owner of the void. The owner was Teun van Dien[8], a policeman whom they had occasionally spoken to in the months since moving to The Hague. Since returning from the front, Willem had already become intensely secretive, and although he sensed Teun shared their antipathy towards the Nazis, he avoided going into detail. There was a vague discussion where nothing specific was said or described, but by the end of it Willem was convinced that

---

[8] Pronunciation: Teun van Dien = *Työn fun Deen*.

he was free to modify the space into a storeroom. Later, Teun was to become a close friend and confidant of the family.

Photographs of the gutted inside of the secret chamber, taken in the 1970s

Willem worked on his pet project all summer. The chamber was small, but that made it inconspicuous; and there were no windows, no plaster on the inner walls, nor even floorboards or lights. The height of the structure was also an advantage: from the outside it was an insignificant part of the original building, and looked like an oversized chimney stack. There were no real shortages of building materials in the first year of the war, and Willem was relatively unhindered as he went about refurbishing it.

Kieks was happy to help, and keen to make sure that he did not make too much of a mess in the adjoining room, which was to be her seamstress's workroom. She was soon moving buckets of rubble out to the back of the

> How he did the room to hide people

house and helping to dispose of it discreetly. Willem fitted floorboards and other primitive furnishings, including long, deep storage shelves across part of the void. He finished the entrance from the boxroom, leaving an opening only about two feet by two feet wide, with its bottom edge some three feet above floor level; impractical for a room, but fine for a secret storage area. Willem fitted a modest mirror over the hole, to provide a concealed entrance into the hidden chamber. The mirror was intended to look like a dressing mirror, so it was the same width as the opening but taller, extending above the opening, and again of a modest size to make it inconspicuous. He mounted the mirror on concealed hinges, with an ingenious catch so that the mirror-door could be opened from either side. As he inspected it, he tapped it; when it was tapped at the bottom it perhaps sounded hollow, but when it was tapped near the top it sounded quite solid. It would have to do. Finally he completely redecorated the boxroom to hide all traces of the work. If anyone searched the house and asked what the room was and why there was a mirror, this was where Kieks worked and fitted clothes to her customers' satisfaction. Downstairs, he modified the bedroom windows and fitted two small mirrors. These he set so that it was possible to stand out of sight from the street and look up and down the full length of the road.

Now finished with her schooling, Kieks wanted to find a job, but with the war in progress, there were few opportunities around. She reasoned that if she didn't have a job of sorts she would end up doing more and more of the housework, so she was excited at the chance to start up a small business taking in sewing work. She was soon able to get some jobs adjusting and repairing people's clothes, which also helped give her a sense of being an adult and contributing to the family household. She was aware that as the youngest, and clearly her mother's pet, the rest of the family did not take her completely seriously. This gave her some privileges, but also reduced the attention she was able to command in family discussions.

During 1940, the first year of the war, the German forces in Holland were preoccupied with establishing their presence. Before the war, each local administration had created a *'Bevolkingsregister'*, a register of every citizen, and now the occupying authorities issued an order that required every citizen to fill in a form that determined if they were Jewish, according to certain criteria. The form was filled in by most Dutch citizens, including the Jews, and it became a crucial appendix to the *Bevolkingsregister*, which now added religion to the record of each individual's personal details.

With these details added to the register, the Jews were officially identified, and the persecution of the Jews would begin within months. By November that year, Jewish civil servants were being dismissed from their posts, and by the end of the year, all Jews had to be registered with the authorities. Once they had registered, their fate was sealed. Now identified as Jews they would experience harassment and progressively be forced to live ever more apart from the rest of the population. Many Dutch folk were unhappy about the treatment being meted out, as the Jews had always been accepted as part of Dutch society. However, the Dutch way of life at the time was for each group and social class to live their own lives in relatively separate communities. The persecution bemused Kieks, who didn't yet fully see the significance of what was happening. In those early times, the harassment, discrimination and exclusion seemed petty and mean rather than the start of an attempt to exterminate a whole race.

Gypsies, blacks and other ethnic groups were also being subjected to discrimination, but not with the same ferocity as was focused on the Jews. Kieks' puppeteer cousin, Guido[9], was concerned about his assistant because of her black skin. He decided to marry her, which immediately gave her a degree of immunity, enabling her to live through the war without much discrimination or persecution, a solution that just would not have been possible for Jews.

Willem was particularly galvanized by a piece of graffiti daubed on the walls of the local prison: 'Lousy Invaders – Get your hands off our rotten Jews', and he talked about it over dinner one night. Kieks felt detached from the developments, seeing the graffiti as trivial gallows humour, but Willem and Martha remembered the images of *Kristallnacht* and were deeply concerned. Willem seemed to be steering the conversation into how they might help Jews, and they talked about their Christian beliefs and the duty to help people in need. Moeder strongly agreed. Her devoted Dutch Reformed faith had guided the family to bible study most evenings and church every Sunday and she felt it was important to act, not just

---

[9] Pronunciation: Guido = *Hwee-doh* (*G* is a guttural *h*).

to talk about the bad things that were happening. However, as the conversation developed, it seemed to drift off into other matters and came to no definite conclusion.

As the Gestapo became more entrenched, they started to hunt for the Jews who weren't so willing to come forward and register. Those they did find were rounded up and taken away. Stories of 'the Atrocities in the North' were spreading across the country, putting an end to the gallows-humour graffiti they had seen, as the Dutch became afraid of giving any hint that they might be supporting the Jews, and began to fully recognise the horror of what was happening in their midst.

In Citroenstraat, there was little change in their routines from that of peacetime. As 1940 rolled by into 1941, Kieks continued to find customers and take in sewing as a seamstress, both to earn some money and to justify having a spare empty room. There were rumours circulating of mass evacuations and people being re-housed in under-occupied buildings. Whatever the truth of the rumours, the family wanted to avoid taking any risk, and were happy for her to fill the spare room with needlework and scraps of material, as evidence to justify a workroom. Kieks was pleased; she liked having a role in the house that was not just housework. Her Needlework Certificate from her recent exam success was flamboyantly hung in the entrance hall of the house as extra camouflage.

Her sister, Trijntje, was dating Dirk, a man from Leeuwarden who now lived nearby. One weekend in May 1941, he went up to visit his father in Leeuwarden. While he was there, he was arrested; apparently the Germans had found his name on a list they had seized in some raid. The family suspected that the list was for the committee of a Christian youth organisation, but that the Germans had been suspicious, thinking it was a cover for the Resistance. As a result, he spent six months in the prison in Scheveningen, and then in October was sent to Kamp Amersfoort, the Nazi concentration camp. Trijntje and the family could do nothing but worry and hope that he might be released soon. Kieks spent a lot of time trying to comfort her sister and they soon became close. In December Dirk was released unexpectedly and came back to Trijntje, shaken by his six months in prison, his personality subtly changed. From that time, any enthusiasm he had for the Resistance evaporated and he kept clear of all underground activities.

Apart from their worries when Willem was called up and away from home, the Okmas had not been affected much by the war. They didn't see any fighting, there had been no bombs or explosions, and the main difference in their lives was the presence of occasional security patrols and the Nazi preoccupation with identity cards. Measured against the words of the Chinese curse, life was interesting, but not too interesting.

This was to change suddenly. One day in late September 1942, there was a knock on the door: Kieks opened it to find a young couple standing on their doorstep. The man was slightly built, in his early-thirties, about five-foot-six, with black curly hair and a prominent hooked nose. He introduced himself as Salomon Hekscher and his wife as Lien. They came from Coevorden, a small town in the Drenthe Province, close to the German border, and had been given Willem's name and address. After a few words, Willem appeared on the doorstep and intervened, quickly ushering them inside. He now had to do some explaining to the family, and his recent preoccupation became clear.

While he had been serving at the German border, Willem had shared a room with a man called Kraantje[10], who had told him of a Jewish family that lived nearby. They were increasingly worried about what the Germans might do to them, and Willem had given Kraantje his address and suggested he might be able to help them in some vague way. From what the couple had said, he was pretty sure that this was why they had ended up at the family's front door.

The Hekschers explained that they had not known where to turn after the Gestapo moved into Drenthe. They had a young child, and had managed to place him in the care of a trusted friend, who had agreed to look after the child as if he was their own. Then the couple had secretly made their way across Holland, in the hope that they would reach Willem and that he might help them find a way to safety.

Willem talked over the situation with his family. They had often discussed what was happening in Holland and how they wished they could do something. Here was a family they could help. The Okmas should shelter them as *'onderduikers'*[11] for a while, until Willem could find a

---

[10] Pronunciation: Kraantje = _Kraahn_-chuh.
[11] Pronunciation: onderduikers = _ohn_-de-day-kers. Dutch: literally, 'under divers'; people of all persuasions who were hidden from the Nazis during the war.

way of getting them out of the country. At the worst, they could keep them here for the duration of the war. It was 1942, and like many people, he judged that it probably wouldn't last more than another six months.

The family talked about it for a while. Kieks was frightened, but kept to the background, listening to her mother and sisters. As the youngest, she was aware that her opinion seldom carried much weight, but she did agree with her brother's plan and would be willing to go along with Willem's suggestion – if that was what Moeder decided. The rest of the family were also frightened, because the Germans had made it very clear what would happen to anyone caught aiding *onderduikers*,[12] and the debate went on for some time, bouncing between her brother, her mother and Martha. They all remembered their previous dinner conversation about the graffiti and the unspoken decisions they had touched on, and this helped them reach their conclusion.

Eventually they all agreed to take in their unexpected guests. The Hekschers were brought upstairs and told that they could stay. Later they were shown the

---

[12] Discovery of involvement in sheltering Jews meant an immediate death sentence.

secret way into the hidden chamber. They were now the only people outside the family who knew of its existence.

Salomon was a cheerful, personable man with a good sense of humour, who could see a funny side to almost anything. Although he didn't find the present situation amusing, Sallie, as he was known, was able to fit in with the family, and his humour became a useful lubricant as he and his wife settled into the role of unexpected house guests. Sallie and Lien had owned a drapery shop in Drenthe, and so shared a common interest with Kieks. She enjoyed their company and the dinner conversations, which became more varied for a while. She little knew how events would unfold for her from this turning point.

Willem started to plan the next step in the Hekschers' journey. He made enquiries about various individuals who claimed to be involved in smuggling Jews out of Holland over to Britain. He was very cautious and suspicious, and became convinced that the people who introduced Jews into these networks were being betrayed by Nazi collaborators[13] and rounded up by the Gestapo.

---

[13] Willem was right. The Henneicke Column infiltrated the Resistance

He heard of three or four people who had helped some Jews and then disappeared, and after this he decided to have nothing to do with the smugglers. The family would look after their guests for the next few months until the war ended. Willem repeated his mantra that the war would probably be over within six months, and this would be the less-risky option for all of them. Kieks was only vaguely aware of stories of people disappearing at this time, and felt happy to accept his word. The family acquiesced.

Soon after the Hekschers' arrival, Willem asked Sallie to adopt a non-Jewish name for the duration of the war. He explained: It was inevitable that the Okma family would want to talk about him in front of other people, and they could not risk being heard talking about 'Salomon'. Salomon understood immediately, and grinned as he said, 'That's simple. I'll be Piet. That is the name of an apostle, and you never hear of a Jew being called Piet'.[14] Lien's name was judged to be safe.

---

networks, tracked down and captured some 8,000 hiding Jews, and handed them over to the Nazis for extermination. They received bounty of 7.50 guilders per Jew. Their mission largely achieved, the group formally disbanded in October 1943, but continued to track down hidden Jewish property for the Nazis.

A couple of weeks after Piet and Lien moved in, a casual friend of the Okmas came to the house. Martha unthinkingly showed him in to the living room where Piet was sitting with the others. The family members introduced themselves: Willem (six foot four), Martha (five foot nine), Kieks (five foot ten) – and 'Piet Okma', a few inches over five feet and about twenty-five pounds lighter than anyone else. The visitor didn't bat an eyelid, but there was a faint suspicion of a smile on his lips.

As soon as the friend left, Willem called a family conference. Most of the family had spotted the smile, and Kieks had been amused by the reaction. Willem's reaction was different; he was very worried about being betrayed, and when they had given thought to his words, Kieks and the whole family agreed: From that point on, they would not invite any more people back to the house. This meant they were also now obliged to stop visiting friends, since they couldn't explain why they weren't returning any hospitality. Kieks and the others were beginning to appreciate the disadvantages of having their guests; this would now disrupt their whole lifestyle.

---

[14] Dutch: 'Pete', for Peter the Apostle.

The family soon realised they couldn't avoid all visits, so Willem came up with a new solution. He fitted an alarm bell, with the button near the front door and the bell upstairs. When anyone knocked on the door, a family member would first press the alarm, and then make sure they delayed opening the door long enough to give the refugees the time to go upstairs and possibly climb into the hiding room. The alarm signal was simple: three short rings followed by one long one; the opening bar of Beethoven's Fifth Symphony, and the Morse code for 'V'; V for Victory, a signal being made famous at this time by the BBC radio broadcasts coming from London.

It wasn't just the family's social life, but their simple living arrangements that were affected. Kieks and the others now started muttering about the difficulties of nine people having to share the one bathroom. With the arrival of the Hekschers, Willem returned to the job of home improvements and fitted a hand-basin in the top bedroom to take the pressure off the single bathroom on the lower floor. It was not much, but for the rest of the war, the household would have to bear the strain of sharing the one washbasin, the one bathroom and the kitchen sink.

Ration cards were now being used, and the arrival of Piet and Lien meant they had to acquire more cards to feed the household, and for this they needed help from the Resistance. Their cousin, Tine van Deth, the police inspector, had been involved in starting Resistance cells, but she was already in jail. Willem knew many of her contacts and so he started making cautious enquiries. The route led back to his sister, Trijntje, and her boyfriend, Dirk. Dirk had a brother, Sjoerd Bakker[15], who was involved in a number of Resistance activities, and Willem went to see him and explain what the family needed. Soon some extra ration cards arrived. Before long, it became part of Kieks' routine to call round to Sjoerd when the need came to collect the next set of extra ration cards for the *onderduikers*.

Apart from Tine van Deth and Sjoerd Bakker, there were other family acquaintances who also crossed the paths of the Nazis, and at least one other spent the war years as a hostage in the main jail in The Hague. This man was much more fortunate and was able to direct his various black-market dealings from within the prison. Part-way through the war he was given a few days home-

---

[15] Pronunciation: Sjoerd Bakker = *Shoert Bukker*.

leave. Nine months later, his wife gave birth and he proudly sent out birth announcements, giving his 'temporary address' as 'The Oranjehotel[16], The Hague', a rather grandiose but unambiguous title for the jail.

A few weeks after Piet and Lien had arrived, a rather flamboyant figure came to the house. Piet Brakel[17] was in his late-twenties, and a member of the local church where the Okmas worshipped, most Sundays. He had a simple question: Would the Okmas look after two Jews who were on the run? It would only be for a short time, there were others who would help smuggle them out of the country. As he spoke, Kieks got the impression that he had launched a personal crusade to help refugees escape from the Nazis, and that he was going round the houses of as many church members as possible and placing Jews with them. Willem didn't believe there was a risk-free route out of the country, but decided not to say anything to avoid hinting at the refugees they were already sheltering. Instead, the family would need to consider it.

---

[16] Dutch: 'Orange Hotel', the popular nickname given to the part of the Scheveningen Prison used by the Germans to intern Resistance fighters.
[17] Pronunciation: Piet Brakel = *Peet B<u>rah</u>-kul*; Joop and Bep van Gelderen = *Yohp* and *Behp fun <u>Hel</u>-der-un* (G is a guttural *h*); Jood = *Yoht*; Wim = *Vihm*.

Another longer family discussion ensued. Moeder was persuaded by the links with the church, and talked of their Christian duty to help, and thus Kieks was persuaded and supported her mother. The other sisters talked of the practicalities, the difficulty in feeding everyone, the sharing of the bathroom facilities. Kieks was aware that she had more time than most of them and that she would help with the extra housework that would inevitably result. Willem agreed with Moeder and even talked of the family's reputation in the church congregation, saying it would seem strange if they did not help. All the Okmas agreed and a few days later another couple arrived.

The couple were Joop and Bep van Gelderen. They had been trying to live inconspicuously in the suburbs as the Nazis tightened their grip on the country. However, by May that year, regulations had been imposed requiring Jews to wear a large yellow Star of David on their clothes emblazoned with the word *'Jood'* to mark them out as Jews, and it was this that had finally persuaded Joop and Bep that it was time to go into hiding.

They had eventually made contact with Piet Brakel, who had seen it as his Christian duty to help. The Van

Gelderens had two young children, a 6-year-old girl called Carrie and a 3-year-old boy called Ernst. One evening, a few days after they had first met him, Piet Brakel's brother, Wim, and his wife, had come to visit them, and had taken the girl, Carrie, away to hide in their home. It had taken them another few weeks to find a second family to look after the son, Ernst, and then the Van Gelderens could make their move. With only the clothes they wore on their backs, they set off with Piet and went to the Okmas. In October 1942, they entered the house in Citroenstraat, anxious both for themselves and their children.

Their arrival meant another change to the routines in the Okma household. The extra numbers required a new discipline in using the secret compartment overnight. The small opening into the chamber was difficult to climb through, and the refugees had to be ready in case a search party were to arrive at the door. From this time on, Willem suggested that at least two, and preferably more, should sleep in the claustrophobic void every night. The shelf that Willem had fitted was deep enough to act as the upper bunk of a bed, and this, plus the space below, became the cramped sleeping quarters in the chamber. Some mattresses were acquired and the shelf became a bed for the Van Gelderens, while underneath, the lower level would be used by the Hekschers. The space had not been designed as a room to live in; when the wind blew, air came in through small gaps near the roof, making the space cold and unpleasant.

For the Van Gelderens, this was a dramatic change from the life they had left behind. From a normal home with their own kitchen and bedroom, they had moved into a space with a cold, dark, claustrophobic cell to share as their bedroom and now obliged to accept whatever food was given to them. They were slightly older than the Hekschers and found it more difficult to adapt to the changes forced upon them.

Kieks explained the situation to Dirk's brother, Sjoerd, and soon got more ration cards to help feed the new refugees. The household now had eleven ration cards, even though only seven Okmas were registered as living there. The cards had to be registered at a local grocer, so five were registered at one and six at another. The family had the advantage of being new to the area, and since other family members such as cousins were often coming and going, neighbours did not know exactly who or how many of the Okmas called this address their home. Now there was also a need to prepare and cook food for eleven people, but to keep the kitchen looking as if it was only catering for seven, and to dispose of the increased refuse without raising suspicions. As the one without a full-time job, Kieks found that much of this drudgery landed on her plate, and she sometimes wondered if perhaps she had been a bit too enthusiastic with her support for harbouring the refugees, although when she thought about the consequences of not sheltering them, she knew in her heart that there had been no alternative. Willem was always checking round the kitchen, making sure that there were no clues as to the extra people in the house, and sometimes he asked Kieks to go out with bags in the evening, to put some of their waste in neighbours' bins.

Joop did not have Piet's easy-going personality and had difficulty adjusting to the way of life in the clearly compromised Okma household. As he settled in after the ordeal of his family's flight and separation, the more trivial things started to get on his nerves. He became preoccupied with the way the Okmas ran their kitchen, feeling they were too casual about food hygiene. Refrigerators were not yet a common household appliance, and sometimes he found milk or food going off after it had been set aside. Whenever there were stomach upsets in the household, he would wonder out loud if perhaps they were caused by the Okmas' carelessness. He also spotted their food stamps occasionally lying around when food was in short supply in the house, and he would express his fractious views firmly when he felt there was a reason to do so. Being the one doing most of the housework, Kieks was the main recipient of these comments and she took umbrage at them; she felt he had no appreciation of how much work was involved in bringing the food in, stretching the meagre rations, hiding the waste, or organising the smooth running of the household under such strained circumstances, and she did not like outsiders criticising the way the family lived their lives. Although the rest of the family shared her views, they were not so intensely irritated; Kieks guessed that perhaps they did not spend so much of their time in the kitchen.

In response to these carping comments, Kieks found herself becoming progressively more assertive, trying to shake off the mantle of being the child in the family, and she increasingly spoke her mind when the pressures of the household built up.

Inevitably, frictions soon started to develop in the household, but Piet and Lien discreetly intervened, acting as a buffer, and keeping the tension to a low level with a tactful use of humour. With the extra numbers in the house, the household polarised into two communities that congregated in separate parts of the house, and the refugees now tended to stay on the top floor, while the Okmas lived their lives in the rooms below. The Van Gelderens felt more at ease in the company of Piet and Lien and accepted the arrangements. As this routine took hold, the four refugees started to spend much of their time playing bridge. Consequently there were fewer conversations with Piet, and Kieks missed them, but she did feel more comfortable when she was free from strangers looking over her shoulder, telling her how to organise the kitchen.

Willem started to worry that there was now an outsider who could link the family to their Jewish guests. He felt that Piet Brakel had been quite reckless in the way he had approached him, and that it was only a matter of time before Piet would be caught and interrogated by the Nazis. The Gestapo were developing a reputation for their skill in extracting information from their victims, and Willem was convinced that if they got their hands on Piet, a raid on their house would be inevitable. He talked to Piet and they agreed that if he was caught, he would try to resist the torture for five days, to give the Okmas time to prepare for a raid. By then they should be ready, and after that, well, there was only so much abuse that a human body could withstand. In the face of the inevitable, the Okmas started to prepare for a possible house search.

A few weeks later, in November 1942, there was another ring at the Okmas' door. Another couple stood there, this time with a 2-year-old toddler in front of them. As soon as the door was opened, the strangers said, 'This is Bram[18]. We think you know where his parents are. It is too dangerous for us to look after him any more'. At this they rushed off, leaving the bewildered child on the doorstep.

Kieks looked down at the small boy. Traces of black curly hair looked as if it had been shorn with a kitchen knife, and below that, a fine-featured face, perhaps

---

[18] Pronunciation: Bram = *Brahm*.

with a prominent nose, again suggested Jewish origins. He was brought up to the apartment where Piet and Lien were sitting. When they saw him they gave a startled cry. He was indeed their son. Lien burst into tears of delight, but Piet was uneasy as he tried to work out how the boy could have been brought to the house. He realised that their friends who had fostered the boy were clearly unable to cope and must have got in touch with Kraantje, the man who had been their intermediary with Willem. That was the only way they could have found out where his parents were hiding. He mused over the way they had left the boy, how they had worked out where his parents were, and the way they had made it clear they weren't going to take no for an answer. He also thought back to Willem's request that he adopt a non-Jewish name, and decided to choose a temporary new name for his son. Young Bram was given the name Jantje[19], after another apostle.

Kieks took an immediate liking to Jantje and was cheered up by this new arrival. She enjoyed playing with him and was pleased to have a new youngest member in the household. In some way it made the job of protecting the refugees all the more important and relevant: here was

---

[19] Pronunciation: Jantje = <u>Yuhn</u>-chuh. Dutch: 'Johnny', for John the Apostle.

an innocent child that the Nazis wanted to kill; there was no question but that they had to do everything they could to protect these people.

In the first few weeks after he arrived, the atmosphere in the town seemed to be relaxed, so Kieks' sister, Ella, took Jantje with her when she went to the crèche where she worked. However, the Nazi hunt for Jews was becoming more pervasive, and when a janitor at the school gave her a kindly word of caution that Jantje's appearance could lead to questions being asked, the family decided that the trips to the crèche should stop.

Ella

At the weekends, Kieks got the chance to take Jantje out for walks in the fresh air. When he was well wrapped up, Kieks convinced the rest of the family that his features were unremarkable and so they could risk letting him go outdoors. The child was too young to need identity papers, but any accompanying adult would, and Lien's papers clearly stated that she was Jewish. Willem refused to let her go out because of the risk of a random security check, and so Kieks got the opportunity to take him with her when she went to collect the household rations. It was one of the household routines that she really enjoyed and afterwards she liked to talk animatedly about the outing to anyone who would listen. Lien found this particularly hard to bear, as she desperately wanted to be out there herself. Kieks made little effort to control her enthusiasm as she described how an excursion had gone, and she was sometimes surprised when Lien reacted badly to stories, concerned that Kieks might be putting Jantje in danger. Kieks was frustrated by these reactions, sometimes feeling that she was being crticised for doing what was best for the child, but she was unwilling to let anyone else do the job.

A few weeks after the new refugees arrived, a man with a strange uniform was spotted coming to the house. No one recognised the uniform, but the red stripe down the side of his trouser legs implied some sort of authority. The man rang the doorbell; as planned, the alarm at the door was rung, and quickly the refugees all piled out of the workroom and into the shelter. After a suitable delay, the door was opened, and the man announced that he was a gas inspector and had come to perform a safety check on their system. The family were suspicious of the stranger, but let him in. He started inspecting the gas fire in the living room, and then the cooker in the kitchen. For a long time he appeared to work quietly, sometimes standing silently peering at some piece of equipment. The others watched him and waited in silence. After what seemed like several hours he announced everything was fine, and left.

The refugees came out of the shelter, cross at having been cooped up in the dark for what they felt had been no good reason. They reckoned it would have been quite safe to sit quietly in the sewing room. Even so, the Okmas remained uneasy about the visitor, convinced he was not what he claimed, and anxiously speculating about who he might be. No one could work out what uniform he was wearing or what organisation he worked for. For the moment they heard no more, and eventually they ceased worrying. But the Okmas were right and the explanation was to be revealed some time later.

Piet had now become the main link between the refugees and the Okmas. He still enjoyed talking with the Okmas, and was intrigued by the differences between their cultures and their approaches to life. Kieks usually enjoyed the conversation, although sometimes she was irritated by the inferences he seemed to draw. When the subject had come round to education, he had asked her what they thought of their father, a man who had benefited from a good education yet had not thought to provide a proper education for his children. For Kieks, her father was someone who had disappeared when she had been only seven, and she often thought about him, holding his memory very dear. The atmosphere with Piet had quickly cooled on that occasion as she defended her cherished memories of her father, but these discussions were part of the day-to-day routine and more often took place without rancour.

Piet seemed to view these conversations as casual exercises in comparing different cultures, and he respected the differences that separated them. His cultural background led him to regard their mother, whom he always called *Mevrouw*[20] or Mrs Okma, as the matriarch of the house, to be obeyed without question, and he voiced his disapproval whenever Kieks argued with her, objecting that she did not treat her mother with enough respect. This also irritated Kieks, who felt it was none of his business.

He was quick to react when he didn't approve of things he noticed. On occasions he had come into a room where Willem and Kieks were sitting close, whispering together, even as it grew dark. On some occasions he felt they were too close, and he would insist on switching on the light and joining them as a chaperone, engaging in conversation to ensure propriety was maintained. Willem was irritated by his stance, but Kieks had mixed feelings: she was certainly offended by the interference, and loyal to the family reputation, but at the same time she did feel a little uncomfortable with how close Willem sometimes

---

[20] Pronunciation: Mevrouw = *Muh-froh*.

positioned himself when they were talking, and the way he seemed to unconsciously let his hand brush against her.

Apart from these minor interferences, Kieks was comfortable with Piet, but less so with Joop, and the presence of strangers, continually appraising, often criticizing and making judgement on their personal life, was a strain not just for Kieks but for all of them. In a city occupied by the Nazis, home was the one place where she might hope to unwind, but that was difficult in this crowded household. As times passed, she was conscious that sometimes petty little issues seemed to be overwhelmingly stressful, and at times she went to read her Bible for solace and to calm herself.

Kieks' second brother, Douwe, was still living in Hillegom, a short train journey north of The Hague. At first, Douwe was not aware of the refugees' presence, but he frequently came to visit and join the family for a meal, and as a family member he felt free to go upstairs and wander around the bedrooms. On one occasion, he was walking up the stairs when he met Piet coming down. Douwe, over six-foot tall, stared quizzically at the small, distinctly Jewish-looking person in front of him. Piet held out his hand and said, 'Hello, I'm Piet Okma'.

Douwe said, 'I don't know you, but I'm Douwe Okma'.

Piet asked, 'Are you going to move in?'

Douwe replied, 'No, I am a real Okma; I'm just visiting'.

Later, when they retold the story over dinner, everyone laughed.

The other brother, Ruurd, lived in Arnhem and was seldom seen by the family. When the war started, he already had two young children, Dirk and Ineke[21], and with the pressures of raising a young family in a time of war, he had become distant from the rest of the Okma family. He had spotted some business opportunities and was now doing well. During the war he never visited, and so never came in contact with the refugees and was only aware of vague details about their presence.

---

[21] Pronunciation: Ineke = *Een-uh-kuh*.

The assassination in February 1943 of a high-ranking Dutch official, who had been collaborating with the Germans, triggered a succession of harsh reprisals. The Nazis stepped up their clampdown by executing the fifty Resistance hostages they had held imprisoned, and launching a series of raids on Dutch universities to search out Resistance cells. This posed an increased risk of exposure of Resistance networks connected to people like the Okmas.

Radios had been banned soon after the Occupation started, but the Okmas had held onto theirs, which they used to listen to the BBC's *Radio Oranje*[22], keeping it in a position ready to be hidden away quickly. There were newspapers, but they were little more than Nazi propaganda, so the Okmas rarely brought copies home. There was little for the refugees to do apart from talking about the past, listening to the news broadcasts, extracting whatever local news and developments they could glean from the Okmas, and playing their never-ending games of bridge. Joop found the routine more difficult to cope with

---

[22] Dutch: 'Radio Orange'; the Dutch-language BBC European Service wartime radio programme broadcast from London for 15 minutes at 9 p.m. every day, playing a major role in keeping the Resistance alive. Managed by the Dutch government-in-exile, it often broadcast the exiled Queen Wilhelmina's speeches to her people.

than the others did, and whenever he ended up as 'dummy' in their games of bridge, he would go down and morosely stare out of the bedroom window. Usually, he would stand at the window behind the net curtain, staring out at the street, but sometimes when he felt it was safe, he would pull back the curtain and put his face against the glass. Joop had very Jewish features, and the Okmas feared someone might spot him and report him. There were stories that this had already happened elsewhere and they pleaded with him, ordered him, to keep away from the window, to stop risking all their lives.

One day, Willem came home early. As he came into the street, he happened to glance up, and saw Joop leaning out the open window, looking at the comings and goings in the street. Furiously, Willem walked to the house and then raced up to the bedroom. He swore and cursed at Joop, telling him 'his big Jewish nose could cost them all their lives'.

Joop was equally furious at being talked to in this way and a blazing row ensued. He was particularly uncompromising: 'You made a choice. You chose to put yourself in danger by sheltering us. We didn't choose. We did nothing, and yet we find ourselves hunted like animals. Don't expect us to feel sorry for you. It is far worse for us than it is for you!'

Kieks and her sisters looked on in horror, taking in the intensity of the moment and the anger in their voices.

Once the shouting had died down, Willem made the situation very clear: The Okmas had agreed to take them in and give them shelter, and they were doing their best to look after them and feed them while the war lasted. The Okmas might wish to be rid of the refugees; the refugees might want to get away from the Okmas; but at this point in the war, that was impossible. If anyone left, they would be in the hands of the Gestapo within hours. The Jews would be shipped to prison camps and the Okmas would end up in jail, or worse. As far as Willem was concerned, the refugees were going to stay in the house until the Germans had left Holland, and while they were there, they would do as they were told.

The house was overcrowded with eleven adults having to live in a four-bedroom house, for months that now looked set to stretch into years. Four could not even go outside, and they had little idea of what was truly being done to protect and look after them. Willem's words had brought to a head a simmering sense of resentment in

Joop at the powerlessness of his position, and the occasion would burn in his memory. Piet eventually managed to intervene and help calm things down, and also made an extra effort to limit Joop's contact with Willem from then on. With that, the intensity of the moment faded.

Kieks had been feeling hostile towards Joop because of his comments about the way she managed the kitchen, and Willem's angry comments resonated with her. The heated sentiment behind his words had encapsulated the seething emotion that she had been bottling up within herself. Once the angry eruption had subsided and the stark emotions of the moment had ebbed away, the biggest impact Kieks noticed was the way in which the mutual trust between the Okmas and the *onderduikers* in the household seemed to fracture and disintegrate.

Shortly after the incident, Willem told the family of news about Sjoerd Bakker, the brother of Trijntje's boyfriend, Dirk. Sjoerd was the family's contact with the Resistance, and from the moment the first refugee had arrived at Citroenstraat, it was he who had been supplying Kieks with the extra ration cards for the *onderduikers*.

Sjoerd was part of a cell of seventeen Resistance workers whose activities had extended considerably beyond ration cards. They had become aware that the Nazis were using the records stored in the Amsterdam *Bevolkingsregister* to collect details of each resident's religion, and they had decided to take action.

On the night of the 27th March 1943, the group had organised a raid on the building and managed to set fire to the files and destroy at least some of them. Sjoerd's role had been to manufacture the fake police uniforms that the raiders used to disguise themselves when they went into the building. Unfortunately, the group had been casual about covering their tracks, making little effort to hide, and going straight back to their homes after the raid. The information had seeped back to the Germans, and now he and most of the others had been rounded up.

The interior of the Amsterdam Bevolkingsregister after the raid by the Resistance

As Willem gave the family the news, he emphasized again the importance of security and secrecy. He now told the family they should keep all news and plans from the refugees, as he was concerned that Joop might do something unpredictable that would put everyone at risk. His paranoia was contagious and Kieks instinctively took on board every word. She looked at Joop in a new light, increasingly viewing him as a possible threat, and brooding about what might happen if there were to be another flare-up. Willem's advice was also adopted by the rest of the family, and was to become their guiding principal for the duration of the war. Secrecy and security now governed their every action.

In July 1943, Trijntje and Dirk announced their engagement. Just a few days later Sjoerd and most of his fellow Resistance workers were executed. Only two of the original group survived. The emotional shock rocked the household, and the Okmas did their best to support Dirk and Trijntje. Kieks had been so excited by Trijntje's engagement, but the news of the death had sucked all the joy out of the household almost as soon as the engagement had been announced.

It was cold comfort, but Kieks was able to reassure the family that their immediate arrangements for ration cards were unaffected, because by now they had other contacts within the Resistance. With that, they had to get on with the routines of life.

Across the road from the Okmas' there was an apartment occupied by three men. The Okmas had suspected from their looks and bearing that they might be Jewish, but the three seemed unconcerned about any threat from the Gestapo and went about their business with no attempt to hide or keep a low profile. Often, loud music would blare out from the apartment and they seemed oblivious to any annoyance they might cause their neighbours. One day the Okmas noticed a Gestapo car outside their house.

Willem and Kieks considered what they could do to find out what was going on and a plan quickly emerged. Kieks set out on her bike. She cycled round the block and rode past the house every so often, trying to see what was happening. Eventually, some Gestapo officers came out with one of the occupants and drove off. Kieks spoke with Willem and they agreed she needed to look through the window to see what was happening. She went up to the house and stepped into the garden to pick a bunch of flowers. With the flowers in her hand, she now had an alibi as a thief and felt it safe to go up and look through the window. If challenged, she was just checking to see if she had been spotted stealing the flowers. The adrenaline was pumping round her veins, and although she didn't feel an immediate sense of danger, she knew that it was extremely dangerous to mess with the Gestapo. Even so, she sensed that God was looking after her and she had faith that He would protect her. Holding the flowers up to her face as a screen, she peered through the window. The place was empty, so she returned indoors to report back.

Two of the three occupants had not been in the house when the Gestapo had raided, and a few hours later, one walked into the street carrying a small day-case. Teun van Dien, the Okmas' neighbour, spotted him and ushered him into his house. Teun suspected that one of the neighbours must have betrayed the group, and was very nervous, fearing that he would now be reported for giving the man shelter. He was convinced that his house would be raided by the Gestapo at any minute.

Apparently on cue, there was a sudden loud knock at his door. Quickly, Teun bundled the man through a skylight window and told him to go along the roof and climb in through the first open window he came to.

Meanwhile, in the Okmas' house, the family were going about their business and the refugees were in the upstairs workroom, keeping themselves entertained. As they sat there, they were startled to find a young man throwing a suitcase in through the open skylight window and then diving in after it, headfirst. He dangled there upside-down for a few seconds before they helped him in. Would they shelter him? The Gestapo were after him! As he looked round the room, he immediately realised that the four other occupants were Jewish *onderduikers*. He was as surprised as they were, and suddenly his face broke into a smile of relief. The Okmas were quickly summoned upstairs, and after a few words, they all went down to the front bedroom and looked out. A grocer's delivery boy was emerging from the policeman's house – it had been a false alarm.

They went back to the workroom and looked out onto the roof. There was now a stranger in plainclothes hiding close to Teun's window, holding a gun, waiting for something to happen. They went back to the front bedroom. As they looked, a Gestapo car swept back into the street and stopped outside Teun's house. The occupants got out and rushed up to his door.

The Gestapo found nothing at Teun's– the grocer's boy had unwittingly saved the man's life. Teun van Dien was taken with his wife to the Gestapo headquarters and kept there for several weeks. He had a cover story: he had seen the man many times in the street without the yellow star that would have marked him out and so hadn't known that the man was Jewish. He and his wife were kept in separate cells. At one point, Teun heard the screams of a woman being tortured, and he feared desperately for his wife, but knew he had to stick to the cover story. After four weeks he was eventually allowed home, and later returned to his duties as a policeman.

For Kieks, the Gestapo's speedy return and investigation emphasised just how high the stakes were in sheltering the Jews. For the moment, the Okmas were now sheltering five adults and a child in their house. If they made one mistake, they would pay a high price.

The surprise visitor introduced himself as Kurt Lewin. He showed them a passport in the name of Christiaan Gans[23] and explained that the owner had given it to him and then reported it as stolen; so he now lived by the adopted name of Chris. Later, the Okmas would look at the passport of the original Chris Gans, and doubt it would have protected Kurt. Kurt had distinctly Jewish features, quite different from the photo in the passport, and in any case, the surname Gans was still seen by some as Jewish. Nevertheless, they accepted his story and invited him to continue.

Chris was an intellectual in his late-thirties, a Jew from Germany, and he told a harrowing story of how he had already narrowly escaped one hunt by the Nazis. He and his wife had been persuaded by a boat owner that

---

[23] Pronunciation: Gans = _H_ahns (G is a guttural _h_).

there was a way for them to escape. The man had offered to take them out by boat to a submarine, which he had assured them would be there to take them over to England.

There had been eight Jews in the planned escape party and they had eventually met up with the boat owner on the quay of Ijmuiden[24], a port on the North Sea, just a few miles from Haarlem. As they had stood there, a forlorn group on the quay, Nazi soldiers had suddenly appeared, with dogs barking and rifles pointing at them. The whole operation had been a trap. Chris alone had run from the dogs and the rifles, and had hidden in a garden in the town. Later, he had made his way to his in-laws in Amsterdam, where he had been sheltered, and had then been passed from one household to another, before ending up in his apartment across the road. The other Jews who had been on that quay in Ijmuiden, including his wife, were all subsequently transported to Poland, and there his wife would eventually be killed.

As they talked, Chris casually pulled a gun out of a pocket. The Okmas stared with horror. This could cost them their lives. As Kieks looked more closely, she saw it

---

[24] Pronunciation: Ijmuiden = *Eye-mow-din*.

had a beautiful mother-of-pearl handle, but the barrel looked suspiciously rusty, making her wonder if it was more of an ornament than a weapon. He talked of using it to defend the household if the Gestapo came, but the Okmas protested strongly. They knew how severe the reprisals could be, and they tried to get him to hand it over. At this point in the war, if the Okmas were found with unarmed refugees, then they might possibly escape with their lives. But if Chris were to do what he threatened, then not only the Okma family, but possibly other neighbours would be shot. However, Chris insisted he was going to hold onto it and eventually they conceded, but only if he promised that he would only ever use it to kill himself – to avoid capture; not to attack Germans. Eventually all was agreed, and Chris stowed his gun away.

The Okmas remained very concerned about the gun, talking about it and worrying that Chris might do something stupid. Nevertheless, they were not prepared to try to take it from him by force. Kieks felt very perturbed about the threat this posed, and found herself looking at all the refugees with a sense of unease. What other surprises were in store?

In the ensuing days, Chris told them about a letter that he had carried during the escape attempt at the quayside. He had first received it while making his preparations for the escape, and it had come from someone he had known to be in the Resistance. It was an important letter with secret information in it, and he, Chris Gans, had been entrusted with it. He was to have taken it onto the submarine and delivered it to an address in London. He had carried it with him to the rendezvous on the quay, and had protected it as he had made his escape. It was waterproof, so not easy to destroy. It was a long, complicated story, ending with him eventually managing to return it to the person who wrote it. Now he worried about it, thinking about what would have happened if the Nazis had captured it.

Willem listened at first, but then dismissed the story, saying he just didn't believe it. Instead, he came up with an alternative suggestion: If Chris was so worried about such a letter, perhaps he had posted one with secrets in it – for example, a list of people who had helped him in hiding? It would have been stupid because everyone knew that mail was intercepted by the Gestapo, but it was a possibility. The Okmas had speculated that perhaps a neighbour in Citroenstraat had betrayed the three Jews because of the loud music, but perhaps that wasn't what happened; maybe the letter was the reason why the Gestapo had raided the flat.

Chris was offended; he was not used to someone doubting his word. He denied this and refuted Willem's suggestions robustly. Willem paused, and carefully hiding his feelings, he sat down and let Chris finish his story. Once he had done so, Willem made his position clear: neither Chris nor any of the others could go out of this house, and they were not to write down the names of anyone who came to the house, they were not to keep diaries, nor try to send any letters to anyone until the war was over.

Kieks had listened intently to the two of them as their argument had started to become heated. It was one opinion versus another, and if she had to choose sides, she would trust her brother over this stranger. But suddenly Willem had seemed to step back, and let Chris tell everyone his side of the story, before bringing the discussion to a close.

Later, he talked about it with Kieks to explain his apparent change in mood. He had realised there was no point in shouting. He had learnt from the previous shouting match with Joop and he didn't want another. Willem had made his mind up about Chris's story and there was nothing that Chris could say that would change how the family should act. So he might as well let Chris tell his story if that led to peace in the house.

Chris's attitude also reinforced Willem's determination to make sure that nothing of their dealings with the Resistance was ever discussed in front of the refugees. As far as the refugees were concerned, the family members went out about their business, and appeared back with the necessary food and clothes for everyone. There was nothing else they needed to know.

The five adult *onderduikers* now lived increasingly as a self-contained group upstairs, while the rest of the family tried to live their lives as normally as they could. During the day, the refugees would gather in the workroom and use it as their livingroom; at night, one or two might sleep in the workroom, but the others had to sleep in the shelter. The shelter was dark and airless; no one liked to be in there. Yet the entrance was small and difficult to climb through; there would be little time to react if there was a raid.

Chris did not get involved with the games of bridge that the other four played, and instead started a routine that had the effect of separating him from the rest of the people in the house. He would lock himself in the family bathroom for long periods while he worked on his papers and notes and apparently became immersed in writing some book. With the bathroom now shared by twelve adults, it was a practice that the others in the house all found both puzzling and frustrating at times. He tried to tell Kieks what he was writing about, leaving her with the impression that perhaps he was writing detective thrillers, and that perhaps he thought they would make him some money after the war. Willem had his suspicions but decided not to make a fuss. On occasions such as these, there was something about Chris – possibly a hint of arrogance – that jarred with Kieks and the other refugees. His response to any personal criticism was often to dismiss it as 'perhaps a bit anti-Semitic', and this would particularly irritate Kieks.

The workroom was laid out as a needlework room with clothes awaiting repair, so the refugees could use it as their wardrobe area; at a cursory glance the clothes could belong to customers or other members of the Okma family. Moeder insisted that the refugees spend the morning keeping it tidy and maintaining its disguise, and it was only after one o'clock that the refugees were free to relax and play bridge or whatever else they cared to do. The world of the *onderduikers* was very small, with limited information coming in and they would inevitably analyse every nuance of what happened in the house, making judgements about the events going on around them over which they had little influence. Eventually the whole top floor of the house became their territory, left undisturbed by the Okmas. They could also go down into the bathroom where they could get washed or have a drink, and from the lower bedroom they could look out onto the street. However, as a security measure, they were discouraged from coming downstairs to the lowest floor, where the Okmas congregated in the evenings.

Kieks reflected on how circumstances had changed. From a selfish point of view, she was disappointed that her workshop was now almost out of bounds, with the layout of her workshop designed to camouflage the presence of the refugees, rather than to provide a place for her to run her needlework business. She had to admit there was not a lot of needlework coming in, and there would necessarily be an increasing amount of housework needing doing with all the extra people present. In some ways, it was the extra housework that she resented more; strangers had nearly doubled the household, and it was the Okmas who had to do the work to accommodate them, with a substantial burden weighing on Kieks' young shoulders.

Moeder was a devout Christian, and respected Piet, a devout Jew. She was less comfortable with Chris, who displayed no strong religious beliefs, and occasionally talked of God as if He were a friend rather than a Divine Being, something Moeder regarded as approaching blasphemy. The refugees always treated Moeder with great courtesy, almost reverance, to the extent that Kieks sometimes felt they treated her as if she had supernatural powers. One occasion in early summer particularly stuck in Kieks' mind.

There was one regular occurrence when the refugees could go outside and get some fresh air. On washdays, the household washing was hung out to dry on the back balcony. Once the sheets were hung out, they formed a screen that shielded the occupants from view, so that they could briefly sit in the fresh air, out of sight of the neighbours.

There had been a long spell of cold, wet weather, and the household washing had not been done for some time. Moeder ignored the sleet falling outside and announced that they would do the washing the next day. As they helped in tidying up, the refugees started to gather sun chairs ready to be taken out onto the balcony the next morning. The younger Okmas looked at them in disbelief. It was sleeting, it was wet, it was cold outside; were they mad to plan on sitting outside tomorrow? Chris tried to explain their actions with a touch of humour. 'God holds Mevrouw Okma in His grace. If Mevrouw Okma says she will do a washing tomorrow, then God will make it dry and warm, and we will sit out on the balcony.' As he finished saying this, his jaw seemed to drop.

Kieks watched him make the joke, and interpreted his reaction as a sign that he recognised his words were blasphemous in the eyes of the other Jews. However, Trijntje reminded her that it was Moeder who occasionally reprimanded him for making blasphemous remarks and it was perhaps her reprimand that he feared.

When the next day dawned, Chris was proved right. The day was warm and Moeder's washing was graced with glorious sunshine.

The Okmas' washing machine was hand-powered, so the household wash was a full-day affair. The whole household worked as a team, sorting, putting pots of water on the cooker to boil, transferring water, turning the handle of the washing machine, working the wringer and hanging out the clothes to dry. First on the line were some sheets, and once they provided a screen, the refugees could go out on the balcony. As the clothes dried, they had a few hours in the fresh air, first helping with the wash and then sitting in deck chairs enjoying the sunshine. They worked cautiously, leaving the sheets hanging at the edge of the balcony and changing the clothes hidden by the sheets, always making sure that there weren't too many sheets or other items to raise suspicions from neighbours.

Otherwise, the refugees were confined indoors, with little to occupy them apart from interminable games of bridge. Young Jantje was unaware of anything unusual in their situation, and pottered around playing his own little games.

Each arrival of new refugees had caused the Okmas to make major changes to their lifestyle, and each time it took a while for the household to settle into a new routine. Willem seemed oblivious to the stresses and tensions, and within two weeks of Chris arriving, he came back to announce that he was bringing in yet another refugee from the Nazis. This one was not Jewish, but was a friend of Truida's fiancé, Jan Boone[25]. The only thing Willem knew about him was that he had been in a German concentration camp and now he was on the run, trying to avoid the Gestapo.

The new fugitive's entrance left Kieks startled and flustered. The man was Gommert Krijger – or Kees to his friends. Kieks had known him before the war, and his arrival sent a sudden flood of emotions flowing through her.

As soon as she was alone with the family, Kieks announced decisively that the house was getting too crowded, so she would move out. There were plenty of other relatives nearby, and she wouldn't have too much difficulty finding a place to stay.

---

[25] Pronunciation: Jan Boone = *Yun Boh-nuh*; Gommert Krijger = *Hom-mit Kray-Huh* (both Gs are a guttural *h*); Kees = *Kayse* (like *case*). The surname Krijger means 'warrior' in dutch.

Willem was aghast, and her mother burst into tears. Willem pleaded with her, and told her she was being selfish in talking of leaving. She was the only one who had time during the day to do all the jobs which needed doing. Without her, the burden would be enormous on all the other family members, and he didn't see how they could possibly cope. Kieks was furious and countered that she should have been consulted before this man was brought round, but Willem dismissed this: she was only a young girl of 20; she couldn't expect to be consulted every time a decision had to be made. This disregard for her made Kieks more upset and she got increasingly angry, accusing him of double standards.

Eventually she yielded to her brother's scolding and her mother's tears, but she felt trapped by the situation and was aware of the further notching up of the tension in the house. Abruptly, the exhilaration of being part of a team had gone and the perception of being a functionary was overwhelming her.

Later, Kieks revealed her feelings to her sister, Martha. She had been out with Kees on a double-date with Jan and Truida just before the war had started. She had found him physically very attractive, but she was unsettled by the overpowering emotions that welled up inside her whenever she was in his presence. She had been delighted to go out with him on that date, but there had been a secret sense of relief when her mother had insisted strictly that she return home on time afterwards. Now she was frightened that she might make a fool of herself in front of the *onderduikers* and the family. She found it hard to hide her feelings, and didn't want any courting to be done under the gaze of the refugees.

Having resigned herself to the situation, the awkward atmosphere triggered by the arrival of Kees soon faded. At times she would still have that rush of helplessness as an overwhelming wave of emotions washed over her when she was in his company, but she tried hard to persuade herself they were just friends under the same roof. She soon noticed that Kees was paying her a lot of attention, which she began to enjoy, and found herself unable to resist responding and encouraging him.

Before long she found herself falling in love with Kees.

Moeder was aware that Chris exuded a certain appeal for some of the girls, and was uneasy with this, feeling that

Chris was paying too much attention to Ella for her liking. She eventually set a timetable for the household routines, with the one o'clock deadline for all the Okmas to be downstairs, for the purpose of preventing the younger girls spending too much time in his company. In the morning, Kieks and Ella might go up into the workroom to do needlework or other chores. Moeder would allow them to be upstairs till the house curfew and then would call them down 'to let the guests have some peace'.

Although the younger girls were prevented from spending much time upstairs, the eldest daughter, Martha, was free to come and go. Before any other members of the family had noticed it, Martha had fallen in love with Chris. As they became close, Martha started passing on messages and doing chores for him. Chris was married with two children, and although his wife had been captured, the children were still alive and in hiding, and Chris had their addresses. Soon, Martha was making regular visits to check that the children were faring well. Kieks shared a bedroom with Martha and so they often talked as they went to bed. Kieks felt uneasy about the relationship, worried that Chris might be exploiting Martha's vulnerability.

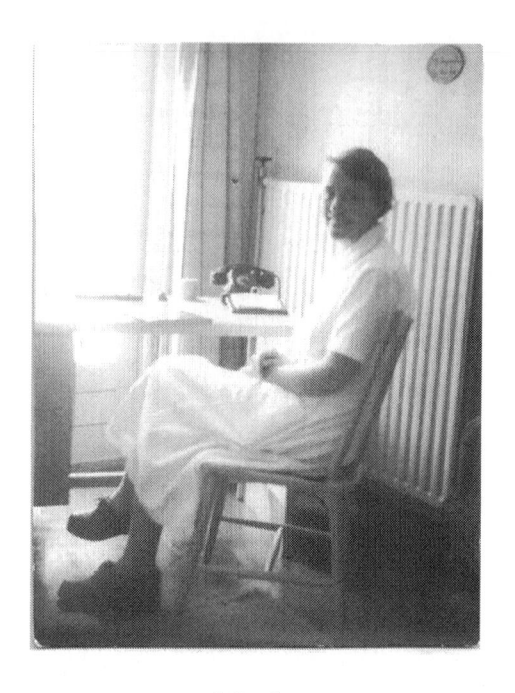

Martha

There were many extra chores needing to be carried out to make the oversized household run smoothly. The rubbish to be disposed of – discreetly, in other people's bins; the ration cards to be tracked, rations to be fetched, with separate family members going to different shops. Most were busy with their full-time jobs, and much of the extra work fell on Willem, Martha and Kieks. Willem and Martha acted almost as head of the family, trying to keep the unit together whilst sharing their house with strangers. Kieks, the only family member without a regular job, handled the contact with the Resistance organisation, collecting the food ration cards and doing most of the extra fetching and carrying that the wartime situation required.

She was frustrated with the role that had evolved for her. She could see that the women in the household were all being kept busy with the day-to-day running of the household, while the refugees, and particularly the men, seemed to spend most of their time lounging around playing cards. She suggested to Moeder that the refugee men should be given a rota to take turns in helping with the meals; preparing vegetables and other time-consuming chores. Moeder agreed, but almost immediately, Martha intervened, insisting on doing all the chores that fell to Chris. Her stance undermined the plan, and with this precedent set, the rota never got started. Kieks was deeply frustrated with the outcome, and protested loudly, but her mother shushed her and there was ultimately little change to the routine.

Since Kees was not Jewish, it was safe for him to go out on the streets, and he explained to the Okmas that he was staying with them simply to avoid the Gestapo, who might go to his parents' house looking for him. His presence and ability to leave the house with her gave them space that allowed their relationship to blossom.

He and Kieks occasionally took Jantje out to the country, where they could escape the tensions in the house and relax, and in the autumn of 1943, most weekends they spent supplementing the household rations by going out to the fields and picking the loose potatoes which had been left scattered on the ground after the harvest.

They were not alone in combing the fields for potatoes, and Jantje's task was to act as guard once Kieks and Kees had filled the first bag. First, Kieks would get Jantje to give the loudest scream he could, her way of warning the other people in the field that this was how he would react if someone tried to take their potatoes. Once the potatoes were gathered, they would pay the farmer, and plan how to get the potatoes home. Before venturing onto the road, they needed to look out for any Nazi collaborators who were on 'Ration Patrol'. These patrols would often stand near the fields, and confiscate the potatoes that people had collected. Instead, the three of them would try to sneak out of the backs of fields, jumping across the ditches and channels to avoid the patrols.

On one occasion the ditch was rather wide, so Kees first tossed over the bags of potatoes and then jumped across. Next, Kieks took Jantje in her arms and threw him over to Kees, before jumping over herself. Jantje never uttered a sound, but Kees cursed loudly as he caught the child. When they got back to the house, Jantje soon burst out: 'Kees used naughty words when Kieks threw me across the ditch!' Piet and Lien were startled and asked for an explanation. They made it clear that they did not approve of the escapade. Kieks enjoyed the outings with Kees, and the element of disapproval gave them an extra piquancy.

In early September 1943, Willem came home with bad news. Their greatest fear had come to pass. On the 5th of September, Piet Brakel had been arrested by the Gestapo and was being interrogated. Although it was almost a year since he had brought Joop and Bep to their house, they now had to assume that he would eventually break down and give the Gestapo their address. Piet had promised he would try to hold off for five days before saying anything, so they had a few days to prepare. Willem called a family conference and they all sat round and prepared plans.

Every possible scenario was considered and everyone was given a set of tasks for which they alone were responsible.

Firstly, they had to prepare a plan of action assuming that the Gestapo would arrive unexpectedly and search the place. If they managed to get over that hurdle, one of them would almost certainly be taken in for questioning. If possible, that would be Willem. He had to have a cover story, and the other family members needed to know it because they would be questioned too, and they needed to corroborate it when it came to their turn, as it inevitably would.

The cover story was simple. They would use the truth as much as possible. Yes, Piet had brought a couple to the house. Jewish? Surely not! Piet must have tricked them. They had stayed for a couple of nights and then had left. Where had they gone? It was such a long time ago nobody could remember – they had just left. As they talked, the name of a local family came to mind. The family had all been executed by the Nazis, and Willem decided that if they were pressed, they would name this family as the probable destination of the visitors.

Kieks joined in the planning, with her mind racing for solutions as the realisation sank in that they were now being forced into perilous and uncharted territory, facing a level of scrutiny from the Gestapo that they had never had to face before. They were hiding *onderduikers* and the *onderduikers* had a gun; punishment would be an immediate death sentence. She was gripped by fear as she thought of all the possible things that could go wrong in a Gestapo raid.

Kieks and the family went through all the rooms in the house, looking for any hint of the Jews' presence that the Germans might spot. They made sure that the amount of clothes and personal belongings matched the number of people who were meant to be living there, and that the other clothes were the type that might be expected for a needlework business. The refugees used Kieks' workroom during the day to relax, so things such as men's socks and toiletries had to be removed. They also checked the kitchen to make sure there weren't any give-away signs there. They could have food and crockery for six people, but any extra supplies or rubbish had to be hidden away.

For twenty-four hours a day someone was stationed by the window on guard, using the spy-mirrors to watch the street; often Kieks or another family member during the day, and one of the refugees during the night, since they had a chance to sleep during the day. Every movement on the street was analysed and discussed. Plans were made about what each refugee needed to take into the secret chamber, and how they would leave the rooms they vacated. Everything was checked and rehearsed. Two refugees stayed in the workroom and the rest slept in the shelter; there would only be enough time for two to squeeze through the opening once the alarm had been raised.

At first, Piet Brakel had managed to pass on a few messages to his family via other prisoners, but he had soon been transferred to solitary confinement. He had resisted the Gestapo torture as long as he could, and had survived almost a full month of interrogation, but on the 5th of October his family received the chilling notice that he had died in custody.

Suddenly in the middle of the night, the Gestapo arrived at the Okmas' door. The warning signal was sounded, the refugees grabbed their things and crammed into the secret room, and the family made a last frantic check as the Gestapo came into the house. Kieks scanned through the workroom at the top of the house – and froze:

The bed-settee had been part stripped, leaving the sheets and a warm dent where one of them had obviously been sleeping. Someone had panicked and had already made the first mistake. Kees was hiding with the others tonight, but perhaps he had not been there when they had rehearsed the evacuation. Shaking with fear, she looked round for another bedcover, then in desperation, pulled a blanket off another bed, threw it over the settee and sat on it. As she sat there pretending to be doped with sleep, all the terrifying thoughts of what could go wrong flooded her mind.

The Gestapo operatives started wandering round and questioning the family about Piet Brakel. One spotted the button for the warning bell, laughed and said, 'Look, I think I've found an alarm bell'. He reached across and pressed it four times, three short, one long – the rhythm of Beethoven's Fifth, the secret code. For a few seconds the Okmas froze.

The Gestapo seemed not to notice the shock on their faces and started to question Willem. With this, the tension relaxed ever so slightly. The Gestapo moved on to question the others, and started a methodical search of the house. In the shelter, the *onderduikers* waited silently. Lien held Jantje tightly; her hand over his mouth to avoid the slightest sound. The Gestapo worked their way through the house, soon reaching the workroom. Behind the mirror, the refugees crouched, terrified, waiting to be seized at any moment. One of the search party decided to test the mirror to see if there was an empty space behind it, and tapped it firmly.

The refugees heard the knock and tensed themselves for the confrontation. Chris clutched his revolver.

On the other side, the man decided that the mirror sounded solid and moved on. Eventually, they finished with the roof space, finding nothing. The *onderduikers* had been holding their breaths from the moment they heard the search party enter the workroom, and now they could slowly let go.

The Gestapo left, taking Willem with them for questioning. So far, everything had gone according to plan.

As Kieks and the rest of the family gathered their breath, Truida broke down. 'I'm so frightened,' she said. 'If they start asking me questions, I won't be able to stop myself, I'll tell them everything.' Kieks and the family tried to reassure and comfort her, but she was petrified.

Willem was kept at the Gestapo headquarters for week after week, and as each day passed, the family's worries increased. Then a policeman arrived on their doorstep and came in to give them their instructions. He told them that they all had to report to the Gestapo building for questioning. Truida was not in, and as the policeman talked, Kieks' mind started racing, thinking about Truida and her fears. When the policeman asked where she was, Kieks spontaneously blurted out, 'She's on holiday; she's away for a few days'.

The surprised look on everyone else's face perhaps made the policeman realise that something was amiss. There were some blurted comments from the others, but he shook his head to quieten them. His reply was ambiguous: 'Well, I'm sure she really needs a holiday; I'm sure she needs to be somewhere far away for a few days. Maybe that will be best for everyone. But everyone else MUST report to the Gestapo for questioning'.

Truida left The Hague for a couple of weeks and the others prepared for their visit to the Gestapo.

The whole family had to go together to the Gestapo building. As they approached the headquarters, the sense of foreboding increased, and Kieks paused and tried to pull herself together. She could feel her heart pumping as she walked. Everything had gone well so far – don't panic! They reached the Gestapo building, and after a short wait, Kieks was first to be brought to the interview room. As she entered the room, the officers were discussing the case between themselves, speaking in German, apparently thinking she wouldn't understand. Kieks couldn't understand German spoken by a native, but she could understand these Dutchmen. She quickly realised that they accepted the cover story and her fear evaporated. Her confidence came flooding back, and she decided to elaborate.

When they started asking questions, she casually explained that she had been away for the couple of days when the visitors had come. Perhaps they had used her bed to sleep in while she was away. She couldn't describe them – she had never even seen them. The Van Gelderens had arrived at Citroenstraat twelve months previously, so the Gestapo probably regarded it as a cold trail. The rest of the family followed in turn and faced the questioning.

Eventually the interrogators were satisfied that the stories were all consistent and they were allowed to return home, except for Willem.

The womenfolk made their way back and eventually reached their street and walked up to the house. As they approached, the *onderduikers* were looking out for them apprehensively, but could tell immediately from their expressions that all had gone well. The relief flooded over all of them and they could now finally breathe a collective sigh as the tension left them, knowing at last that the enormous shadow had lifted.

Kieks felt utterly elated, mentally chalking up another victory over the Gestapo. When it had come to the crunch, it had been much easier than she had been expecting. It gave her a new sense of confidence. The others had faced much more probing questions and were deeply stressed by the experience. Kieks realised that although she had escaped lightly compared with the others, the stress had affected them all.

Willem was kept in custody a full six weeks until he was allowed to go home mid-November. He was very shaken on his return, and said very little about what had happened while he was detained. He did explain that he had tried to act as a simpleton. It had worked most of the time, but he had almost betrayed himself on one occasion when the interrogators had come into his cell in the middle of the night. Suddenly roused from his sleep, he had reacted angrily and out of character, raising their suspicions briefly.

Everyone was relieved when he finally returned, but the experience left them shocked, stressed, and there was no thought of celebration. They were nearly paralysed by the strain, and the house was pervaded with the anxiety that if the Gestapo ever came back, they would not be able to pull it off a second time.

Immediately after the raid, Truida moved out to get away from the family home and spend more time with her fiancé, Jan Boone. He lived just a few yards away in a side street, close to the Okmas' so she joined the family for occasional meals, but now her base was at Jan's apartment.

By the time Kieks returned to the house from her Gestapo interrogation, Kees had also moved out. Moeder had suggested he move out immediately after the Gestapo raid, but Chris had argued against that, just in case the house was under surveillance. With his move, Kieks had mixed feelings about his departure; a certain degree of loss but also a certain degree of relief, as her emotions still made her feel almost claustrophobic when he was around. Now their every move was no longer under the gaze of the whole household. He had moved only a short distance away and called round to the house quite frequently, so she still saw him often, and he was still in regular contact with Jan Boone and her brother, Douwe.

Douwe, in Hillegom, worked in the local administration, and at a fairly early stage in the war, he had taken up the task of forging papers for the Resistance. The forged documents were items such as licenses and special passes, and these were available to the rest of the Okma family if they wanted them. However, Kieks had never seen originals to compare them with and was nervous about using them. He also produced rail tickets, which she was less reluctant to use. The task of printing was quite a complex and major undertaking, and Douwe was as paranoid as Willem about security and secrecy. As winter closed in, Kees and Kieks started to spend more time with Douwe and Teun van Dien, the Okmas' neighbour. They worked with Douwe, helping him with the printing, the hiding of the printing press and distributing of the printed papers.

Between them, they identified a set of perhaps half-a-dozen safe-houses where Douwe could work. He regularly dismantled his press, ready to move it from one place to another. They would break it down into as many small parts as possible and melt down the lead letters, then carry the various parts around the streets, popping in to visit friends and leaving small parcels here and there for short periods of time. Kieks felt a flush of excitement return, with a little thrill of achievement every time a move was completed and the press was back up and running.

Kees also planned the distribution of the printed papers, and Kieks was quickly roped into those activities. Her task was the apparently simple job of delivering messages and newssheets, but even this could be complicated. Kees would bring her to a street and tell her to walk along it and make a mental note of where all the letterboxes were, so that she could deliver a letter to each one when it was dark and the street lights were off. On the occasional winter evening she would be given a bundle of about a hundred leaflets to deliver. One specific person in the hundred houses was waiting for this letter, but she was not to be told which one. The printed message would be bland and insignificant to everyone but him, and since everyone nearby received a copy, it wouldn't incriminate their man if he was found with it in a future Gestapo raid. She was warned never to bring any copies back to the house in Citroenstraat, and to wash her hands as soon as she had delivered them all. The letter was printed on an old-fashioned copier that required a strong solvent to produce its copies. If the Gestapo caught her with the letters, or even if they smelt the chemicals on her hand, she would be in serious trouble.

She was excited by the adventure, aware of the risks, but had a gratifying sense of achievement every time they completed a round. She felt she was doing at least something for the war, and as she had never been challenged by the Nazis, it boosted her confidence and confirmed her sense that 'God was protecting her' in her good work.

Back in Citroenstraat, life went on. Willem was still an inspector of meat, and just before Christmas 1943, he managed to steal a suckling pig off the production line at work. He took the pig, with its skin covered in swastikas, wrapped it in a cloth, then covered it with an oily rag and put it in the bottom of his tool-bag. Finally he covered it with a layer of tools. When the time came to go home, he took the bag and walked towards the exit. As he approached, he realised there was a spot-check in progress, with the guard looking into everyone's bags. He hesitated, but decided that it would be more suspicious to step out of the search line, and so brazened it out. The guard looked in his bag, checked the tools, and waved him on.

When he got home, he proudly showed everyone in the house his trophy, and the whole household celebrated his achievement. Everyone was offered meat from the trophy, although Piet discreetly declined to eat the 'unclean' meat. The feast cheered everyone up in the household, including Piet, and made Christmas a little more special than they had expected. However, after the close call with the guard, Willem did not have the nerve to try it again.

The Gestapo raid in Citroenstraat had a dramatic effect on Jantje. Disturbed by the tension in the house, or possibly traumatised by the way his mother had held him so tightly with her hand over his mouth during the raid, he now started screaming during the night. There were no other children in the area and neighbours were starting to remark on his presence. Willem began to worry that they might be asked to explain why a young child was heard crying in their house, and Kieks added to the worry, convinced that Jantje's features were looking more and more Jewish.

One day, a neighbour, who was well-known for having German friends, called round to say that she would be having some visitors the following day, and they should 'please keep that child quiet'. This triggered a quick family discussion. Kieks felt it was time to find him a new home, and that she was the best person to take on the job. The family agreed, and she started asking friends and cousins. They moved him out to a friend's house, but this was not permanent, and soon Kieks found herself shuttling Jantje to another house and then another. For several weeks Kieks left him with families for a few days here and there. In some cases, the families said it was too dangerous, in others, Kieks knew they were active in the Resistance and she was worried that Jantje might be picked up in a possible Gestapo raid.

One couple looked after Jantje for several weeks. Wil and Wim Spaans[26] were cousins of the Okmas, and members of the same church. While Jantje was staying there, Wil and Wim had their own infant christened. Everyone went to the church, and since it would be impractical and conspicuous to leave Jantje behind, he was brought along too. Afterwards, there was a reception at the house, with a photographer to record the event. He took one particular photo of the baby, together with Jantje and another child looking over him. Kieks managed to get a copy a week later and brought it back to show Piet and Lien. She was aware that Jantje had been away from his parents for several weeks by now, and she was convinced they would be pleased and relieved to see the photograph.

Instead, they reacted angrily, objecting to Jantje being present at a Christian religious ceremony. Kieks was taken aback by their reaction and responded vehemently. She tried to explain how risky it would have been not to bring him to the christening; it would have drawn

---

[26] Pronunciation: Wil and Wim Spaans = *Vihl* and *Vihm Spahns*.

attention to him. Being at a christening was not contagious, she told them, and they should be grateful they had a photo of their child and could see how he was faring. As she talked, she became conscious of her increasing willingness to stand up to people when she felt inclined to express a different point of view, especially if she felt they were being unfair in some way.

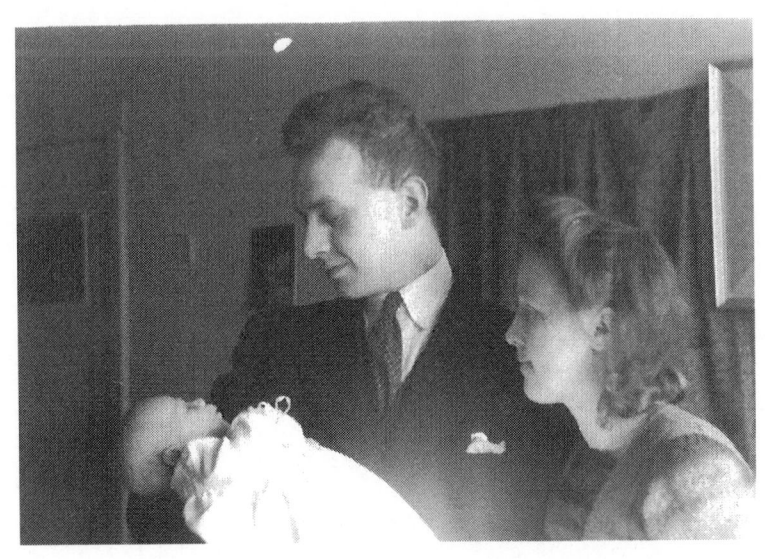

Wil and Wim Spaans with their child at the christening

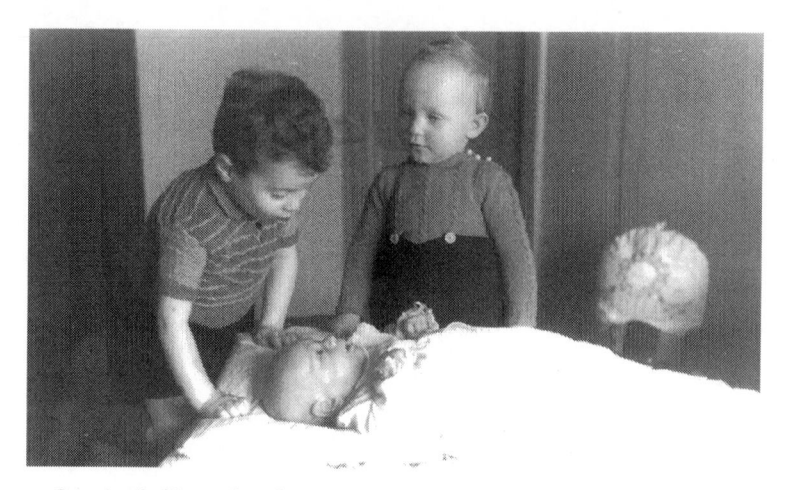

Jantje (left) at the christening of Wil and Wim Spaans' son

After the distress of the Gestapo raid and Willem's detention, life seemed to return to what passed for normal.

Kieks and Kees had been working ever more closely together in helping Douwe with his printing; Kieks found herself increasingly relaxed in his presence, just revelling in his company. They had become increasingly close, and on January 17th, Kieks and Kees celebrated their engagement with a party at Citroenstraat and invited some friends round to join them. Before the party, the *onderduikers* locked themselves in the workroom, to make sure that no guests could accidently wander in on them during the merriment. Everyone shared in a celebration meal of rabbit, with a fiery spirit to toast the couple in the evening.

Kieks spotted one of the guests trying to engage in a conversation with Willem. She recognised the man as a senior member of the Resistance, but as soon as Willem saw who it was, he wouldn't listen to a word the man had to say and hastily started to usher him out of the house. It was then that Kieks suddenly realised that after his brush with the Gestapo, Willem was at that point unable to face the thought of working with the Resistance.

Kieks intervened and walked with the man to the door and as she did, she pondered over the family links with the Resistance. She was very conscious of how much they relied on them for their food and money, and she also realised that she, more than anyone else in the house, seemed to have escaped lightly from the mental stress that had affected everyone else in the family in the aftermath of the search.

As the visitor made to leave the house, Kieks impulsively offered to work in place of Willem. The obligation to repay the Resistance on behalf of the family was something she could explain to Moeder and the others, but she was also attracted by the thought of getting away from the domestic drudgery and replacing it with some excitement and adventure. She would be involved in the Resistance effort on her own terms as a young woman, and not as a child swept along by the family's decisions.

Kieks' offer to help was welcomed and she was soon called on to perform small tasks. She knew that Kees already had links with one group in The Hague, but in this separate activity, the instructions for Kieks were to come from a different shadowy figure.

At that first brief meeting, she was told to expect phone calls telling her to meet 'at the usual place'. This meant she was to go to a particular park and feed the ducks on the left-hand side of the pond. She was to look only at the ducks as she fed them and not look round. After she was given these instructions, her controller would only ever contact her by phone. As events transpired, she was not to see or meet her contact again for almost a year.

Several days passed before she got her first assignment. One afternoon, she was cooking lunch for the household when there was an urgent phone call. The phone message was terse: 'Get to the usual place with your bike, NOW!' The line went dead immediately.

Her pulse started racing. Quickly, she turned off the cooker and announced she was going out. When the others asked where she was going, she replied she was off to feed the ducks. She was conscious of the surprised looks as she hurriedly took a few pieces of bread and left. It was exciting to replace the tedium of cooking the family meal with an adventure for the Resistance.

She got to the pond and started feeding the ducks. As she stood there, a man came up behind her and quietly talked to her. She wasn't to look at him when he left. He was going to put a white envelope in her hand. She was to keep it out in the open and make her way to the central railway station. There were two men across the road who were going to follow her, and they would recognise her by watching for the bike and the envelope. She glanced across and saw two burly men casually looking across at her. She guessed they might be soldiers or saboteurs. She was to avoid any places where identity papers were being checked, because the men didn't have any. When she got to the station she was to put the envelope in her pocket and bend over her bike to adjust the lights. Kieks interrupted to say that she didn't have any lights. The terse reply was: 'Well, fix your brakes then'. Someone would come up behind her and take the letter out of her pocket. She was not to look round at him either, but she could then go home.

She took the envelope and started walking with her bike along the road, taking detours to avoid known checkpoints. In addition to the German soldiers and Gestapo, she had to watch out for the *Landwacht Niederlander*[27]. This was the auxiliary Dutch police force set up by the Germans in 1943 to control and round up Jews and subversives. They would often set up mobile checkpoints to examine identity papers, and they had a reputation for heavy-handedness.

Suddenly, she saw a *Landwachter* car driving up behind her. Flustered by the sight of it, she brought the envelope up to her face as a warning sign and turned to look into a shop window. The car sped by and she turned round to see if her covert companions were still there. The street was deserted; not only had the two men disappeared, but so had everyone else.

---

[27] Pronunciation: Landwacht Niederlander = *Lund-vuht Nay-der-lund-er* (guttural *h*).

Thinking about it later, she could only assume that the two men had run for cover when they saw her reaction. In these tense times, the sight of two men running for cover might have made people panic, and that could have cleared the street. For a while she wandered around, trying to catch sight of the two men. At last they spotted each other and she set off again. But now she had become disorientated and was completely lost. After more walking, she eventually arrived at the station. The thirty-minute walk had taken almost two hours. She leant over her bike, as she had been told, and soon heard the sound of footsteps approaching behind her. As she continued to look down, she was convinced that the shoes she saw were those of a policeman. When she straightened up, the envelope had gone. After this episode, she was not called upon to act as a courier again for some time.

Kieks was still working with Kees and Douwe, moving the printing press and distributing papers. She also still had the task of moving Jantje from house to house, and these journeys were increasingly stressful. It came to a head one day when Kieks was taking him to a family by train and there was a spot check of identity papers on the journey.

Jantje was too young to need papers, but Kieks worried that his features would give him away. Almost instinctively, she quickly took the boy's hand and put his thumb in his mouth, gently spreading his fingers to cover his nose and face. When the guard came to her, she promptly produced her papers, engaging his attention. Once the guard had gone, she jumped up and did a little dance with Jantje to celebrate their success, but stopped dead as soon as she realised the other occupants were starting to stare, and quickly sat down. As the train journey wore on, she contemplated how much the situation was putting her on edge; usually when she was on her own, she would make a point of fumbling and taking time to search for her papers just to mildly irritate the guard. This time had been different.

When they got to the station, they found themselves standing near a young German in uniform looking very dejected. To Kieks' horror, Jantje went up to him and threw his arms sympathetically round the young man's waist. The man looked down at Jantje and across at Kieks, and a frown seemed to cross his face. She was convinced from his expression that he recognised Jantje for his Jewish looks, and caught her breath. He paused, then brushed Jantje away and returned to his own thoughts.

When Kieks got home that night, she talked over this and other risky incidents with Willem and her mother. They all agreed that something had to be done to find a more permanent solution for Jantje, but none of them could come up with any ideas. Eventually Willem suggested she should ask Kees for advice. Moeder thought this was a good idea and Kieks was always eager for a chance to see Kees, so it was decided.

She soon met up with him and raised the problem of looking after Jantje. Did he have any ideas? He pondered for a few moments and was quick with a suggestion. Just before coming to Citroenstraat, he had visited Dordrecht , a town some fifty kilometres to the south east of The Hague. There he had come across a farm labourer whose daughter might help. The girl also happened to be called Jantje, and was an unmarried mother with a one-year-old baby. She lived with her baby and family in a small shack in a place called Willemsdorp. The shack was built on the land between the dyke and the water, a no-man's land where her family didn't have to pay any ground rent or tax. They scraped a living by keeping a few pigs on the surrounding land. He smiled as he added that hiding a Jewish child with a family keeping pigs might even give the child an extra layer of security.

Kieks travelled to Willemsdorp with young Jantje. She talked at length with the girl, and discussed how she might look after the child. Eventually, Kieks offered her fifty guilders a month to do the job, a sum she had already agreed with Kees on behalf of the Resistance. The girl became quite enthusiastic, and told Kieks she would claim Jantje as her own child, fathered by a German soldier. Kieks would act as a go-between, bringing the money and relaying news back to Piet and Lien. It was the first time Kieks had offered money for Jantje's upkeep, and at last it seemed to secure a more permanent home for him.

As she left, she felt a welcome sense of relief. Travelling around with Jantje had become draining and increasingly risky. She also felt a strong sense of responsibility towards the young mother; her family was clearly very poor and she would need every penny of the fifty guilders to care for him. She had made a promise to the girl and, as she walked away, resolved that she would make the keeping of that promise her top priority for as long as the child was in the girl's care.

Soon after Jantje arrived, the young mother's own child became sick. She took Jantje and locked him in a separate room before the doctor came, concerned that he might realise that the child was Jewish. She did not believe that the doctor would betray them, but felt that the fewer who knew about Jantje, the better. It was an act that Jantje was to remember for a long time.

Once Kieks had placed him with the family, she continued to visit them every few weeks, checking he was well and bringing the money from the Resistance for his upkeep. The visits themselves were fairly uneventful, but the house was a couple of hours' bike ride from home and she was occasionally a bit careless about giving herself enough time to get home before the 8 p.m. curfew.

On one visit, Jantje's foster mother mentioned to Kieks that he had developed a cold and was feeling a bit miserable. She asked Kieks to find out from Lien if there was any little treat that he especially liked and might cheer him up. They had a good gossip and Kieks set off, knowing it would be tight getting home before the curfew. Some distance from home she got a puncture and knew at once that she would be late.

She hid behind bushes and waited. Immediately after eight o'clock the roads were swarming with patrols. She knew how serious it was to be outside at this time, and wondered if she might have to stay in hiding till the morning. However, the number of patrols slowly decreased and by ten the roads were deserted and silent. It was so quiet that she was convinced that she would hear a patrol vehicle long before the occupants would see her. Eventually she plucked up her courage, got back on her bike and cycled on to Citroenstraat, closely hugging the roadside and ready to jump behind a bush if she heard any sound of a patrol coming along.

When Kieks got back to Citroenstraat, she was scolded for taking such a risk. To deflect the criticism, she ignored the comments and instead told Lien that Jantje was ill, and asked if there was anything she knew of that might comfort him. Lien got very anxious and soon burst into tears. The others in the house asked a few questions and soon decided that the child was not seriously sick and scolded Kieks for upsetting Lien. Kieks, her feelings hurt, now also got upset, pointing out all the things she was doing for Jantje, and claiming that no one ever seemed to be interested in how he was doing. As Kieks went to bed, she found herself shaking, and realised that she had been more deeply stressed by the experience than she had realised when she arrived home.

A few weeks later, Willem raised a new spectre in his conversation with the rest of the household. He had heard of another Jewish lady who was having difficulties in her present hiding place. He might have to bring her to their house to stay here. Joop was unhappy at the prospect, reassuring Willem that the family had already done so much to help Jews and *onderduikers* for more than the past year. They shouldn't think of doing any more and putting themselves at further risk. Kieks turned on Joop, accusing him of just being selfish and worrying that another refugee would put him at more risk. Joop denied this and continued to insist that the Okmas had done more than their bit. Willem said little in response, but no new visitor came.

Even in wartime life must go on, and on 9th February 1944, the Okma family celebrated a double wedding as Willem and Diny[28], alongside Trijntje and Dirk, got married in one large and cheerful ceremony.

Wedding of Diny & Willem (left) and Trijntje & Dirk (right), February 1944

After the wedding, Dirk and Trijntje set off to live in Groningen, up in the north of Holland. Kieks was happy for them but saddened at the same time, as she felt closer to Trijntje than to any of her other sisters, and realised that she was losing a confidant as well as a sister.

Diny, Willem's bride, moved into Citroenstraat. With the war in progress, Diny and Willem were starting their married life in a shared house full to the brim with ten others. Diny was now part of the family, although she did not completely join in with the Okmas' family life. She

---

[28] Pronunciation: Diny = D*ee*-nee.

kept her own ration card and got her own food, and this did have the advantage that no one raised questions as to the number of ration cards linked to the Okma address. However, it also emphasised the gap between her and the others in the house. Kieks was not close to Diny, and in fact everybody in the household apart from Willem seemed to have a strong dislike of her. As she settled in, she became increasingly assertive, making life unpleasant for the refugees with her sharp tongue, and proving to become an increasingly unpopular member of the Okma household.

She was also free with her opinions of the Okma family members. As the wife of the only man in the household, Diny regarded herself as having extra rights and privileges, and seemed intent on persuading Willem to get the rest of the family to acknowledge her new position. Kieks felt she was possibly most in Diny's firing line, as she did most of the housework. She became convinced that she was being unfairly picked on after a continuous tirade of cutting remarks, and complained to Willem. Willem naively tried to improve matters by telling Kieks what little habits of her own that she could change to make things better between the two of them. Inevitably, this only angered and incensed Kieks further, worsening matters. There were some attempts to improve the atmosphere between the two, but trying to pacify these personality clashes was particularly tricky under the full gaze of the refugees. Kieks suspected that the family arguments might be providing an entertaining floor show to brighten up a dull day, and so found it difficult to express herself freely in these situations. She felt that Diny's domineering presence had made the household atmosphere even more stressful and argumentative.

Kieks was still involved with other Resistance activities in The Hague, and was still pleased with the chance to get away from the tension in the house. The local Resistance fighting group had become involved in operations involving the Special Operations Executive (SOE), a British Special Forces organisation formed in 1940 to conduct espionage, reconnaissance and sabotage missions aiding the Resistance movement in Occupied Europe. The organisation had an almost mythical status with the Germans and was sometimes called 'Churchill's Secret Army'.

The SOE operatives would be parachuted in from England, and the Resistance group's job was to meet them at the drop point and provide them with a safe base from which to launch operations. Usually, they would take over a house for a night or two before moving on to the next.

Kieks' role was to act as housekeeper, sorting out the domestic chores, such as moving furniture to create some space, bringing in and preparing food before they arrived, then returning after the men had departed to clean up and dispose of all the rubbish into other people's bins. She would never meet the operatives face-to-face. The cooking, cleaning and shopping was much like the work she did in Citroenstraat, but there was no bickering and no one there criticising her every move. She could also muse over what the other team members might be doing, although she would never have a chance to learn whether her musings were accurate.

The Resistance were unaware of a deception that the German military intelligence, the *Abwehr*, had managed to set up shortly after the fall of Holland, when they had penetrated British Intelligence, successfully pretending to be part of the Dutch Resistance. This *Englandspiel*[29] was a deception that spanned several years, succeeding in the German capture and control of many of the Resistance Wireless Telegraph operations, which resulted in the *Abwehr* often receiving advance warning when SOE agents were to be dropped into Holland. The *Abwehr* would first let the agents roam round Holland for a few days, using them as bait to identify the Resistance members to the Gestapo, who would then close the net to catch as many as possible. It was a deception that was to affect Kieks directly.

It was early June 1944 and the operation started like any other. Kieks went into the designated house and stocked it up with supplies, preparing a pot of stew for a meal, setting out bread, and then disappearing back into the shadows. Parachutists were dropped over the rendezvous point, collected by some of the men from the Resistance unit and brought to the safe-house. They were housed and fed for a few days and then planned to move on. Once the coast was clear, Kieks was to slip back to the house to clean it and hide any signs of the visit.

But before then, the Gestapo made their move. Within a few days, the parachutists were captured, tortured and executed. As usual, the Gestapo tried to keep

---

[29] German: 'match against England'.

a slight distance from their bait to avoid arousing too many suspicions, and so fortunately Kieks was not near the house when it was raided. The rest of the men from the Resistance group were less lucky.

She was swiftly contacted by her commander, who warned her about the Gestapo raid, and that some of the team had been captured. She paused to think through how she had managed to keep herself at a distance from the rest in the fighting cell, and finally reckoned that the others would not be able to describe her. With this thought, she worried a bit, but persuaded herself that she couldn't be linked to the operation. However, a few days later she was contacted again and told that a rough description of her was being circulated; she was on the Gestapo's wanted list.

The exciting but risky adventure had suddenly become deadly. Now she felt very uneasy and terribly frightened. She wasn't sure if they had actually seen her or if someone had betrayed her. She was unusually tall for a girl, and in the past had found it to be an advantage when she towered over some of the German soldiers or security officers, aware that her height seemed to unsettle them. Now it just helped to mark her out; they had only to look for tall girls and she could be caught. She clung onto the hope that she had managed to keep enough distance from the others so that they couldn't clearly identify her. She was now on high alert for any signs of trouble, changing her routines and avoiding some of her past haunts. Perhaps it was time to go away for a few days.

Events were also posing a challenge to Kees. One day in June, a man named Teus[30] had appeared on the doorstep of the house where he was staying. He had told Kees that it looked as if there was a traitor in his Resistance unit and he, Kees, together with the whole group, was being betrayed. Events unfolded rapidly, the traitor who 'had been told too much' had informed on almost the whole of Kees's team in The Hague. Everyone he had identified was quickly arrested or killed by the Gestapo. Things were getting dangerous. The Resistance reacted, a shot had rung out and the traitor was dead. Kees decided it was time to move away from The Hague.

He moved back to Dordrecht, where there was a network of rivers with many barges and boats still moving

---

[30] Teus was the name given to the man by Kurt Lewin in his diary. Pronunciation: Teus = *Työs* (like *Tues*day).

cargoes to and fro. There, he linked up with a Resistance group that lived on the boats, and soon was enjoying the camaraderie of the group. He had an exuberantly extrovert personality and his behaviour made him the centre of attention, so at first he got on well with the others there. Things soon changed.

Kieks had decided that it was sensible to spend a few days away from Citroenstraat, and she headed off to Dordrecht to pay Kees a brief visit. It was a straightforward train journey, and with the developments in The Hague and her description being circulated, the fifty kilometre journey seemed a suitable distance to go.

She soon met up with Kees and heard about his falling out with the local group. He told her that one day he happened to casually beckon to someone with his finger. Suddenly, one from the group turned and accused him of being a spy. The Dutch way of beckoning is like the English way, with the back of the hand to the ground and the beckoning finger pointing upwards, but the German way is to have the back of the hand to the sky and the finger pointing downward. Kees had made the gesture the German way.

There had been uproar in the group and he had been challenged to explain. After a long discussion he was able to quell the immediate hostility, but the incident had raised suspicions, and suddenly he found he was treated with caution; no longer trusted or let out of sight of the others. As a result, he found himself with little to do and nothing that could be called 'working for the Resistance'. He suspected, though, that no one else in the group was doing much either.

Kieks headed off back towards The Hague and travelled the further forty kilometres on to Hilligrom, where Douwe was still active in his role as a printer and forger for the Resistance. Train tickets were one of his specialities, making travel easy for Kieks. However, he was finding it difficult to organise the moving of the printing press around the countryside and needed help. He remembered how Kees had helped him before and so he asked Kieks to find out if Kees could come and help once again.

She headed back to Dordrecht. Kees had left Kieks the address of a farm near Dordrecht where he might be contacted, and when Kieks arrived at the farm she found him there with a group of friends.

She started to talk about Douwe. As she did so, she sensed the atmosphere of suspicion that seemed to hang over Kees, and decided to take the initiative. Improvising as she went along, she elaborated about the background to Douwe's problems, filling in a bit of detail so that the group could overhear, and at the same time using words to imply she was gently reprimanding Kees, reminding him in front of his colleagues that the Resistance had tasked him to sort out a problem up north, and the need to carry out some 'special duties' with a man up in Hillegom, ninety kilometres to the north. This clearly impressed the rest of his group and she felt she had persuaded them that he could be trusted.

Kieks was delighted at how effective her little charade had been and gave her confidence about taking the initiative, and of her powers of persuasion within the group. However, unknown to Kieks, Kees had been given a challenge that would test his ingenuity and ability to fight the Gestapo.

Kieks headed straight back to Hillegom after visiting Kees. A few days later, Kees contacted Kieks to say he was in the neighbourhood, and asked her to go over to a house near

Hoofddorp, some twelve kilometres from Hillegom, to act as housekeeper. He had been challenged to try to rescue some fallen comrades. Two Resistance members had been injured in an incident and had been taken by the Gestapo to a police station in the centre of Hoofddorp a short distance from Amsterdam. They were still there and were being kept in a small room, watched over by an armed guard.

Kees organised a small group who carried out the task. With careful timing to avoid patrols, they casually strolled into the police station, and once inside, quickly overpowered the two guards, stripped them, gagged and bound them, and put them in the prisoners' beds. They then dressed the injured men,[31] in the guards' uniforms and walked out, propping up their colleagues with a man at each side as they contrived to nonchalantly make their way out of the police station. How much help they got from the police inside was never discussed.

They left the police station without anyone noticing and were brought back to the house, where Kieks took on the job of nursing them, tidying them up, and changing

---

[31] Karel van Boesnack and Hein van Staveren, escaped on 11th August. Pronunciation: Karel van Boesnack = _Kah-rul fun Buss-nuck_; Hein van Staveren = _Hiyn fun Stah-fer-en_.

them out of the guards' uniforms. Soon afterwards, she helped move them on to another safe-house elsewhere, where they could receive further treatment. She did not know much about first aid, but doing this gave her a particular degree of satisfaction: she had helped save them from the Gestapo torturers, from the fate that Piet van Brakel had faced when he had been tormented into giving away details of the refugees in the Okmas' house. The thought made her feel she was making a difference.

Kees was very pleased with how the operation had gone and almost immediately afterwards he was given the job of leading the Resistance group in nearby Haarlemmermeer, about ten kilometres from Hillegom. It was a good location, close to Douwe and so an easy place for Kieks to come and visit. Within a few days, a small group moved into the area to join him, and he started directing operations, which included working with Douwe. Kees quickly showed his organising skills, getting the print distribution underway as well as many other activities. He was extremely well organised, and soon the Resistance cell in Haarlemmermeer was humming with activity.

Soon Kieks took the train back to The Hague and returned to Citroenstraat. As she travelled, she prayed that perhaps the Gestapo had given up looking for her in The Hague. She had kept out of the way; spent a few days in Doordrecht, a few days with her brother and a few with Kees in Haarlemermeer. The Gestapo had probably moved on to deal with other more important matters.

Within a couple of days of her return, she was walking along with her bike in the early evening, when she sensed that she was being followed. She continued to push the bike along, and then turned onto a path through a short patch of woodland that led to another road a hundred yards away. She knew the path well and as she went round a corner, briefly blocking the view of the men following her, she darted towards a large rhododendron bush a short distance from the path, slipped round behind it and into its canopy with her bike. There was plenty of space for her to stand there, and in the fading light she was invisible to passers-by. She looked back where she had thought the men were following her, and sure enough, the two of them came into the wood, now trotting after her, then coming back and looking round, puzzled as to where she had vanished.

When they soon disappeared, she stood there for a while longer. She was shaken. She had to stop being so blind. They were looking for her. Unless she did something, it would just be a matter of time before she would be taken away and interrogated. Suddenly, her confidence was evaporating.

As soon as she got back to Citroenstraat, she talked over the incident with her mother and Willem. She hoped that they would reassure her that perhaps she was just overreacting. Instead, they both became just as alarmed and scared as she was. This appeared to be an organised hunt by the Gestapo; she needed to escape to somewhere safer, to move away for more than just a few days. Kieks was frightened and keen to get away, but also torn by her feelings of duty to the family and the household. How would they manage without her? She still remembered her outburst when Kees had arrived, and how intensely Willem had argued that they could not survive without her playing her part in keeping the household together. She wrestled with a feeling of guilt that perhaps she was exaggerating the risks because she wanted to get away from the tense atmosphere in the house. Whatever her feelings, the day's events had changed things. There were too many warning signs to ignore.

Kieks agreed with Moeder and Willem that she should move out of The Hague and go to Douwe's house for a longer stay, well away from any local Gestapo who might have her description. Kieks was anxious and uneasy, feeling guilty at the thought of how appealing it was to leave the household with all its tensions, and go to one where she was treated with respect, as an equal. However Moeder reassured her, persuading her that she had done her share and it was now time for the other family members to do their bit. An unspoken thought in Kieks mind was that she also knew the move would bring her closer to Kees.

On the last day of August, Kieks took the train to Hillegom. As she sat on the train, she reflected over the events of the last few days, realising just how lucky she had been, and musing over quite how dangerous it was being part of the Resistance. It was no longer just a perilous adventure, but at the same time she felt that the people of Holland were surely compelled to do something to fight the Nazis and protect the victims of persecution. It was definitely the right thing to do. As she contemplated all that had happened and all the dangers, she felt sure that God was looking after her. The journey itself was uneventful, and as soon as she arrived, she made her way to Douwe's house, letting herself in with the spare key hidden at the back of the house. She didn't know it then but the progression of the war would lead to that passenger train being the last one to leave the Hague for a long time.

Douwe and Tiny were pleased to see Kieks return and made her welcome. Tiny assumed that together, they would be able to watch the war developments at a distance, listening to broadcasts from England and picking up snippets from Kees and Douwe's own Resistance contacts. Kieks was relieved to be away from the house in Citroenstraat and just an anonymous girl once more, but she knew in her heart she would soon want to get out into the fray and do something useful.

A few days after her arrival, a German soldier appeared at the door. He told them that he had been ordered to search all the houses and commandeer all bicycles. As Kieks began showing him round, Douwe whispered to her that she should avoid going to the attic, where the bikes were hidden. Kieks led the way from room to room, throwing the doors open to show there were no bikes. Suddenly, as she swung one door open, she saw a radio sitting on a table. Radios were strictly prohibited and they could be shot for having one. Quickly she pulled the door closed, announcing: 'See, no bike here', and marched to the next room. She sensed the soldier hesitate, as if he had spotted something out of the ordinary but couldn't quite be sure what. Even so, he continued to follow her to the next room. She never could decide whether the soldier had shown compassion, or had just sensed there was something out of place but couldn't spot what it was; his mission had been to look for bikes, not radios. After the soldier had left, she complained to Douwe about his carelessness, but he just laughed.

The experience left her with an odd sensation of precariousness. Once again she had escaped what would have been almost certain arrest. She was reminded of earlier occasions where she had felt that God had been looking after her. It was an eerie reminder that the war produced a hazardous lottery; sometimes she did things that were risky, but sometimes the risks appeared out of nowhere and with no warning. Recognising how close she'd come to danger, she was grateful that, with some quick thinking, again fortune had been on her side.

After the landing in Normandy in June, the Allied invasion was well under way. Allied forces had moved up towards the Rhine, working their way towards Arnhem. On the 5th September – *Dolle Dinsdag* or 'Mad Tuesday' – several of the Resistance groups around Holland concluded that the time had come for a final push, and came out into the open in a coordinated move to fight the Germans. Some of the local population thought that the Allies were about to win the war and started celebrating imminent liberation, while others feared that they might soon be labelled collaborators. As a result, many tried to climb on the bandwagon and hastily join the local Resistance groups. The railway workers also added to the chaos by going on strike, almost completely stopping Nazi industry and supply routes.

The Allies launched Operation Market Garden, an attempt to advance to the Dutch border, and on the 17th of September, British forces parachuted in to try to seize the bridges at Arnhem, Nijmegen and Grave. The bridges at

Nijmegen and Grave were captured and much of the region liberated, but the Germans managed to counter the attack at Arnhem, and then dug in to repel the Allies from the northern parts of Holland, setting up caches of arms and ammunition in readiness for further fighting. The Resistance groups were caught out by the sudden change of rhythm; many individuals had now shown their faces in a way that meant they would no longer be able to merge back into the routine of civilian life until after the war was over. The strike by the railway workers added to the pressure on the Germans, but they brought in their own workers and then bided their time, preparing to punish the Dutch population with reprisals for the uprising.

Kees had been given the job of Resistance leader in Haarlemmermeer only a couple of weeks before *Dolle Dinsdag* and found the sudden changes unsettling. He explained to Kieks that with the recent turmoil, many of his contacts and sources of information had gone into hiding, or were in Gestapo hands. After the news of the Allied advance and the events of *Dolle Dinsdag*, strangers were appearing and calling for help or asking to join the group. His usual ways of checking up on individuals no longer worked, and Kees was convinced some were double agents. Everyone now feared betrayal, and as Kees struggled to filter the new faces who were coming forward or were being recommended to him, he was aware that he was making a number of enemies. In spite of the chaos, he was determined to press on and do everything possible to disrupt the Nazi operations.

He decided on an operation to cement his reputation, and sent a message to Kieks. The message told her to go to an address in preparation for an important operation. The address turned out to be Kees's house, and Kieks gladly moved in.

Kieks was much happier and more at ease here, away from the house in Citroenstraat, and being with Kees without an audience watching and judging her. She felt as strongly as he did about fighting the Nazis, and wanted to do anything she could to help. When he explained what he wanted to do, she dived in, working with him to plan the logistics and sort out the arrangements at the house. She was soon bringing in stocks of food and arranging the house for his next operation.

Once preparations were complete, events started to unfold. On the chosen evening, a series of groups of two or three men arrived at the door, every fifteen minutes or so. Each group had their own precise arrival time and was shown to a separate room, where they were told they would have to wait for a little while until the plan could be put into effect.

As housekeeper, Kieks prepared the food and brought each group their share, noting carefully how they responded to her every visit, chatting about nothing as they waited for action. If any one of them were to show any sign of curiosity about whom else was there, or what the plan was, she was to report it to Kees. Any behaviour that even hinted at a possible spy or double agent, and he would call off the operation. Kieks could see how important it was to get this right, and this key responsibility gave her assurance that she was making a more valuable contribution than she had been back in Citroenstraat. She was part of the team and respected for it. It was a much nicer atmosphere.

Kieks recognised a number of the individuals as policemen from the surrounding area. Amongst the others, there was one unfamiliar face, a man calling himself Kareltje[32]. Kareltje told her that he was a German Jew who

---

[32] Pronunciation: Kareltje = <u>Kah</u>-rul-chuh.

had come to Holland just before the start of the war, and was proud that he could speak in perfect German without an accent, if challenged. He claimed he was only 15 years old, but had managed to get papers describing him as a 27-year-old Dutchman. He told Kieks how he liked to mix with the German soldiers, picking up snippets of news and sometimes spreading a little malicious gossip of his own. He claimed he could get into the public baths when they were reserved for the exclusive use of German soldiers, brazenly joining them for a swim. There he did not have to worry about clothes or uniform. He claimed that when he left the baths, he had sometimes managed to steal a gun, which he did primarily to confuse the soldiers. His logic was that this would sow seeds of distrust, and perhaps even cause the soldiers to steal each other's guns. He claimed he had collected five revolvers by the time this raid was being organised in Hillegom. Kieks was not sure how much to believe of his stories, but she enjoyed listening to him.

The focus of the operation was to be the farm sheds that lay out in the fields near the village, and Kieks was to be given the chance of playing an active role, not just the usual one of housekeeper. She was thrilled at the prospect. Before the war, these long-neglected sheds had been used for drying out tulip bulbs after the harvest, but now the Germans had recently commandeered them and had positioned armed guards outside them. Kees's team had discovered that they were being used to store weapons, ammunition and fuel, and Kees had a plan.

The tulip sheds had back doors that opened out onto small canals – little more than overgrown, water-filled ditches. These doors were out of sight from where the sentries stood, and were not separately guarded.

Kees's plan called for a small diversionary charade, which was why he had asked Kieks to accompany him as his partner. It was the first time she was to fully take part in an operation in the field and her heart was pounding as they set out. As called for in the plan, the small lanes close to the sheds suddenly became the haunt of a courting couple, one shed at a time. With a few giggles, laughs, and fumblings, the couple made sure to make enough noise to attract attention, but not so much as to cause alarm. Soon the guard would walk over from the hut, as much to stretch his legs and alleviate the boredom as to investigate. While he was distracted, someone else from the Resistance team could creep up to the back of the shed and carefully oil the hinges of the doors at the canal side, working on them until he could open them silently. Once he had done this, he quickly checked out the contents of the cache and left. Over a few evenings, as they went from one shed to the next, the couple became more intimate and physical in their courting, and the guards became quite preoccupied as they left their stations to get a better view. Apart from being acutely aware of the unnerving presence of onlookers, Kieks immersed herself in her part, enjoying every moment.

The next part of the plan depended on the unwitting cooperation of the Germans. The Gestapo and the Dutch police worked closely together, even though many of the Dutch police were also members of the Resistance. The two forces had separate garages where their car repairs were carried out, but if the German repair shop was full, the Gestapo would take their car to the police workshop and expect theirs to be put to the front of the queue for immediate attention.

Soon after the Resistance men had gathered in the house, Kees revealed that a Gestapo truck had been brought to the police garage. The workshop staff told the

Gestapo it would take a few days, and were given the truck's papers. They had immediately contacted Kees and told him it was available for a few nights.

Some of the Resistance men moved to yet another house, owned by a sympathiser who was away on business. He had a safe alibi, and enough damage was done to the house to make the entry look like a burglary. The house had an attached garage with an inspection pit, important for their plan.

That evening the courting couple gave a particularly captivating display, much to the delight of the guard, who moved as close as he dared. Meanwhile, the Resistance workers, made up of Kareltje and a number of Dutch policemen all dressed in German uniforms, climbed into the German truck at the police garage. They drove it away and took it to a position a short distance from a shed, where a bend in the road hid it from direct view of the guard.

A small punt was taken to the ditch and punted up to the shed. The doors were opened noiselessly and the punt was slowly loaded up with ammunition. For over an hour Kees and Kieks distracted the guard, while the punt shuttled quietly between the shed and the German truck until, at last, the truck could take no more. It was driven off past the guard, back to the safe-house. The courting couple's work done for the night, they arrived back at the house first. A few minutes later, as Kieks looked out of the window, the truck stopped outside. The men got out and silently pushed the truck up the drive and into the garage. The contents were unloaded into the inspection pit, and then the truck was silently wheeled out and finally driven back to the police workshop.

Over a couple of evenings, two sheds were emptied, before the truck then had to be returned. However, there were other sheds ready to be emptied, and later in the war Kees would change tactics. Again using the courting couple as a ploy to distract the guards, he would get his team to enter the sheds and remove just the jerry cans of fuel that were part of the hoard. These would be taken out of the sheds, and simply buried under the mounds of bulb fibre that were piled up beside the bulb sheds. He guessed that when the Germans discovered the fuel was missing, they wouldn't think to search through the piles of debris right beside the sheds.

After the operations were finally finished, the rest of the team quickly dispersed, while Kieks remained to tidy up the house where the weapons had been hidden. She took extra care, washing down every surface that might have been touched to remove every hint of incriminating fingerprints. The operation had been a thrilling escapade, but for the entire duration she had been verging on shaking with fear that something might go wrong and they would be discovered by the Gestapo. As she finally left the house just before dawn, she was relieved that it was over but also acutely aware of the adrenaline coursing through her veins and the tremendous buzz of exhilaration.

Fears that the Germans might have infiltrated the Resistance continued to grow, so operations were regularly abandoned and code names continually changed as the effect of betrayals became evident and key people were mysteriously captured or arrested. Kees became increasingly worried and discussed his apprehensions with Kieks, wondering whether they should risk planning some more big operations.

The high price they might have to pay for being involved hit home a few weeks after the raid, when the one person from the earlier operation that Kieks had got to know, Kareltje, was cornered in a Gestapo raid. The story Kieks heard was that, as he scrambled across the rooftops trying to escape, a shot caught him. He fell to the street, dying. Deciding to make an example of him, the Germans had left his body where it lay, with a guard nearby to stop anyone trying to remove it. It was left there for several days, rotting.

Kees was increasingly troubled by the thought that his group might have been infiltrated by a traitor, and he talked to Kieks about the earlier events at The Hague that had surrounded the collapse of his previous group. He didn't want another group jeopardised by betrayal. He pondered on a recent spate of arrests, which seemed to point to spies in their midst.

A few weeks after *Dolle Dinsdag*, he asked Kieks to act as housekeeper for another operation. She carried out her usual duties, bringing in the food and chatting to the people about nothing much. One of the team passed the time by asking questions about her contacts and whom she worked with. She made light conversation, but alarm bells went off in her head and she asked herself: Was this a man who wanted to have her shot? She went straight back to Kees to alert him, and half-an-hour later he announced that he was calling the operation off and everyone was to go home.

The first operation where they had succeeded in stealing the weapons had been completely successful and undetected. However, the Allied forces had been halted in their advance and there was no battle for the Resistance to fight, and no use for the ammunition. A few months later, Kieks would hear that the Germans had been shown the location of their stolen arms cache – still hidden in the inspection pit. By then, so much else had happened that she was not greatly surprised. Later in the war, the German tanks did start to run out of fuel, and when Kieks heard this she was pleased and hoped that perhaps their work might have contributed at least a little to the shortage.

Haarlem Resistance operatives, Peerke (right) and Remus[33]

As the local commander, Kees was often consulted when problems arose. Activities at a local lock-up garage caused problems on one occasion. As usual, the first that Kieks knew of this was when she was asked to go over to a local

---

[33] Pronunciation: Peerke = *Payr-kuh*; Remus = *Ray-mis*.

house and then given a briefing to help prepare two men for a visit to the Gestapo headquarters.

She asked what was going on, and was told a strange tale. One of the two, Peerke, owned a lock-up garage which had been searched at random by a Gestapo officer. The garage was quite clean, apart from one box casually lying in a corner, but when the officer had looked in it he had found a handful of small, round glass vials with strings coming out of them. The Gestapo officer had frozen when he had seen them, recognising them as the explosive fuses used by the Resistance. He had immediately asked Peerke what they were. Peerke had recognised them but had denied all knowledge, claiming he didn't know, and suggesting they were probably harmless pieces of string. He had pointed out how the garage was only used occasionally and how easy it could be for anyone to break in, use the tools, and leave without trace. He had offered the vials to the officer and suggested he might throw them in the bin if he didn't want them.

The Gestapo officer had seemed as unsettled by the suggestion as by his discovery. The fuses had been a good find, but he had realised he also now had a problem. This type of fuse was notorious because it was so unstable.

They were liable to explode if knocked, particularly if they were warmed up by body heat. It was said they sometimes even exploded spontaneously. What should he do with them? The officer had taken some notes, and decided on his plan.

He had ordered Peerke to take the devices to the Gestapo headquarters in town, and had left. Peerke could see the logic. If he didn't hand in the vials, then the Gestapo officer could easily track him down, because he had taken a note of all Peerke's personal details. Conversely, if he did try to hand them in, then he would probably blow himself up in the attempt.

Peerke was left in a quandary: either to go on the run or to brazen it out. Kees suggested the latter and helped them plan their moves. The team first stuffed his shirt with thick pads of cottonwool to provide insulation, with Kieks using her seamstress skills to make sure his outfit was properly shaped and looked unremarkable. Then they chilled the fuses in a fridge. Finally, when they were ready to go, they put the fuses in the insulated pouch inside his jacket.

Remus and Peerke drove to the centre of Haarlem and then started walking. Remus took the lead, walking in front of Peerke to make sure that he was not accidentally jostled, and the two continued in line to the Gestapo headquarters at the Town Hall. Remus walked normally but Peerke walked tentatively with a strange hunched posture, trying to let the vials drop away from the pressure and heat of his body. As they reached the office, Remus peeled away from the lead, and Peerke adjusted his gait and walked breezily into the office.

Once he reached the reception he flamboyantly took the fuses out of his inside pocket and placed them down on the desk as heavily as he dared, explaining that 'a Gestapo officer told me to bring these things here', but that he didn't know what they were. Later, he claimed that when the soldiers in the office saw what they were, they had almost dived for cover and had all rushed out, evacuating the Town Hall. They had been quite convinced from the way he had handled them that he had no idea what the fuses were, and once they had checked his story with the Gestapo officer, they had let him go with little fuss. He suspected that the Gestapo officer might have had a little more explaining to do.

The series of events seemed to roll continuously from one to another, demanding, tiring, yet exhilarating. Kieks was sufficiently removed from the action that she didn't feel the constant chill of fear, but she was highly alert to the risks and was careful never to discuss events with anyone other than Kees. She was still staying with Douwe, but saw Kees frequently and whenever he came to discuss an operation or talk with Douwe about arrangements for the moving and use of the printing press.

As they continued to work together, Kieks and Kees started to talk of what they might do together after the war, when it finally finished. When he put his arms around her, she felt secure and confident of the future. They were in love. They would always look after and support each other, and neither one would keep any secrets from the other. Kees was often on the move but left Kieks the address of a farm where he often stayed. Kieks could cycle over there; sometimes the trips would be fruitless because he was not around, other times he would be there for her.

In between events, Kieks was still regularly visiting Jantje. On one visit, she arrived at the shack to find Kees and a colleague who was staying there. She recognised the man as one of the Haarlemmermeer Resistance group, but from the way Kees was behaving, she sensed something was wrong. The friend, Joop, seemed unusually curious to know who was Jantje's father and who was the father of the other child, and as Kieks stood there she realised that Kees was giving deliberately vague answers to the questions. She acted as if she knew nothing about the children, and soon Kees and his colleague departed. The prying unsettled Kieks and she reflected on what needed to be done. She resolved not to let anyone else in the Resistance organisation know about Jantje. This meant she now would have to take on the challenge of raising the monthly money herself, as well as getting it over to his foster mother.

A few days after Kieks returned from visiting Jantje, she was called to look after a house, and watched as two of the men from the team were loading up a small truck. They had some heavy bags, and as they passed her, they shook them and asked her to guess what was in them. The bags made a heavy metallic sound but she had no idea. They laughed and told her that they were off on a trip, but would tell her when they got back.

They disappeared but never returned. A few days later she was told that they had been carrying the parts of a heavy machine gun, and had set off in their truck on a mission. Driving along a road they had been surprised by a spot check, and, determined to avoid arrest and torture, they had accelerated towards the checkpoint. They had been shot at and the lorry had overturned, killing them both. Inside the truck, the Germans found the parts of the gun. They were concerned to discover that the Resistance had such heavy weapons and a large number of soldiers were brought in to search the area.

At the end of October, Kieks took a phone call. It was Kees, and he wanted to meet her, urgently. When they met he said he wanted to say goodbye. Kieks asked him what he meant, and he told her a confusing story about now knowing who was betraying their group and that he was going to have to kill him. Events would come to a head at the wall of the St-Bavokerk, a church in the centre of Haarlem. Kees was going to follow the man, and if his suspicions proved to be correct, he would have to shoot him. He was convinced he would die in the operation or would be caught afterwards, and he reckoned it would be better to kill himself rather than to be captured. He was deeply worried about the likely consequences, reminding her of the vicious Nazi edicts about reprisals.

They talked of a story that was circulating. Two officers in a nearby village had started to quarrel over some issue, no one ever found out what. The quarrel had escalated, and suddenly one had pulled out his gun and shot the other. The officer had immediately blamed the Resistance for the shooting, a simple way to deflect the blame from himself. Because of the edict specifying reprisals, he had then ordered a handful of local inhabitants to be rounded up and shot. Whatever the truth of that story, this shooting that Kees was planning would have consequences.

Kieks felt a wave of fear seize hold of her, and as they talked intensely she was shaken at how much Kees had changed. The events of the war around them were changing their personalities, impacting their actions and affecting how they responded to events. She had never before heard him talk of killing a man, and after he had done this deed, she knew things would never be the same again. She told him they had to continue the struggle and continue the fight, and that Kees was crucial in keeping the whole team working together. She couldn't let him just kill himself; that would be giving up.

Kieks spoke to him firmly: He mustn't get caught and he had to plan his escape and make sure he got away. No one else could hold and organise the group the way he had, and he would incriminate too many people if he were caught. There were now over sixty in this Resistance group, and he had responsibilities to all of them. He had to stay alive.

In late October, Kees carried out the mission. From the shadows, he shot and killed the man; the deed was done. Kees escaped to safety, but within a few hours the reprisals began. Ten members of the Resistance were taken from prison, put against a wall and shot, and four houses were razed to the ground. Everyone in the group was shocked and very depressed. Some of them managed to get their hands on a few bottles of gin and got very drunk.

After the war, it transpired that Kees Krijger[34] had assassinated Police Inspector Fake Krist.[35] The man was a collaborator, driven by ideological support for the Nazi

---

[34] The Dutch surname, Krijger, translates as 'Warrior'.
[35] Pronunciation: Fake Krist = _Fah_-kuh Krihst; Cor van Stam = *Kor fun Stum*.

cause, notorious for his success in detecting and arresting Jews and *onderduikers,* and for his reprisals against the Resistance. The shooting took place in Haarlem on the 25th October 1944.[36] The events were slightly different from the story Kieks had been told, which may have been because Kees's commander, Cor van Stam, had told him to change his target and go for the Inspector, or it may even have been because Kees had disguised his plans to avoid betrayal.

Following the brutal reprisals, there was a dramatic slowing down of Resistance operations.

---

[36] See http://virtueletochten.noord-hollandsarchief.nl/?pp_id=115&pc_id=20 for more information. The assassination was the subject of the 1986 Dutch movie *De Aanslag* (*The Assassination*), which received the Oscar for best non-English film. See http://www.imdb.com/title/tt0090576/

Kees (Gommert Krijger), left, with two colleagues who helped him assassinate Fake Krist

Fake Krist, shot by Kees in Haarlem, 25 October 1944

The Church of St Bavo in Haarlem, with the memorial to the ten Resistance fighters shot in reprisals for the killing of Fake Krist

As the war continued towards the end of 1944, conditions became harder. The invasion of Normandy had started in June and the Allies had swept across Europe, rapidly approaching Holland. After the Dutch railway workers had gone on strike, the Germans were now retaliating by blocking all but their own supplies from being moved by rail. This meant that food was no longer being brought into the cities, supplies had plummeted and shop shelves were becoming bare. Now there was practically nothing to be had, and everyone in the cities lived with the constant nagging pains of hunger during the long *Hongerwinter*[37], when 18,000 people would starve to death. Foraging for food became the main preoccupation for almost every city-dweller.

Under the pressure of the Allied invasion and damage to supply routes, the German Occupation became increasingly brutal, with the previous Nazi routine of arrests followed by long interrogations now steadily replaced by summary executions. The Germans also made good use of propaganda to turn the people of Holland against the Resistance. Accidents and apparently bungled sabotage attempts were reported as being caused by the Resistance, with publicity given to the locals who had been injured or killed. In some cases Kieks knew the Resistance had had nothing to do with the events, but she had to keep quiet when friends complained about them. The propaganda started to work, and people in the community who had previously supported them with a bit of food or shelter, became frightened of them, calling them dangerous hotheads, accusing them of causing as much trouble for the Dutch as the Nazis.

---

[37] Pronunciation: Hongerwinter = *hong-er-vin-ter*. Dutch: 'Hunger Winter'.

In The Hague and other cities, the Germans had begun carrying out random raids on houses in their drive to abduct slave workers and send them to Germany. They would cordon off an area and transfer any able-bodied men off to German factories. Trijntje's husband, Dirk, was co-opted into one detail, but managed to escape. He stole away from Groningen with Trijntje and travelled down to The Hague to join with the others hiding at Citroenstraat, now *onderduikers* themselves.

Kieks kept up her routine of visiting Jantje to check on how he was and to pass on the money to his foster mother. On one visit she again got a puncture, well away from any house. It was close to the eight o'clock curfew time, so she got behind a hedge and hid till about nine-thirty, when the patrols had quietened down. This time, she cycled on until she came to the house of a family acquaintance, and knocked on the door. There was a long wait, and then it was cautiously opened. When she was recognised, she was welcomed in with relief and invited to stay the night. The man was sheltering some student *onderduikers* who were hiding to avoid being drafted for forced labour in Germany. They had quickly tried to hide when she had knocked, assuming that anyone calling at that time must be part of a German search party. In later years, the man reminded Kieks of the incident, which for him had been the most frightening event of the whole war. When he had told her this, she had been lost for words.

Although Kieks was still staying with Douwe, she kept in touch with her mother and the family with regular trips back to Citroenstraat on her bike. The *onderduikers* taking shelter at Citroenstraat now included Bouts[38], a policeman who had been involved in smuggling guns for the Resistance and was now on the run.

On one visit, Kieks was chatting with Bouts and the conversation drifted round to the topic of Kees. He told her of an occasion when he had been walking along the road with Kees, carrying some papers. Suddenly a group from the *Landwachter* had appeared from nowhere and had started checking all the identity papers. Without explanation, Kees had grabbed Bouts by the arm and, holding him firmly, had shown the officers a pass and had been immediately waved through. After they had walked a distance, Bouts had insisted on seeing what Kees had shown the security officers. It was an old *Waffen SS*

---

[38] Pronunciation: Bouts = *Bowts*.

security pass for an armed member of the Nazi 'Protection Squad', made out in Kees's name. Bouts had inspected it closely, and had become convinced it was genuine, not a forgery. Kees had eventually confirmed this and had told him a story about having been in the *Waffen SS* and later fleeing from a concentration camp. Bouts did not go into details, but warned Kieks to be careful; there was something that didn't add up about Kees's story.

Kieks didn't believe him, but was troubled by what he had said, and the next day she went to Kees's father who lived a few miles away. He confirmed the story about Kees having been in the *Waffen SS* and talked about him having turned against them. He even pulled out some photos of Kees in his *Waffen SS* uniform.

Kieks was bewildered. Still incredulous that Kees could have been a collaborator, she decided the only way she could sort this out was to talk to Kees. She made her way back to Hillegom and soon met up with him. When she confronted him, he paused, then nodded and told his story. He was quite proud of what he had done.

He explained that at the outbreak of the war, like many, he had been keen on what he had read of National Socialism as it was presented at the time, and had been inspired to join the *Waffen SS*, the secret corps of local volunteers that the Nazis had set up in all the countries they occupied. After a training course in Germany he had been given a job in a concentration camp. It hadn't taken long to become increasingly appalled at the way the Jews were being treated. He had become disillusioned and disgusted by what he had seen happening around him. What he had seen had had the opposite effect to what the Nazis intended. It had brought home to him starkly how Jews were no different from anyone else. He could see that they were simply the victims of bullies, and were being used as scapegoats for everything and anything.

However, the *Waffen SS* was not an organisation you could choose to leave, and so he had stayed, opting to work secretly from inside the organization to help the Resistance. He had been caught passing on the addresses of guards to the Resistance and, after a short hearing, had been sent to a different concentration camp as a prisoner. Fortunately, the staff there had not been told exactly why he was imprisoned, and he had persuaded them he had only committed some minor technical offence. There, he had been given duties as a medical orderly working in the hospital area of the camp and had earned some privileges.

He had got to know and help a group of Chinese prisoners, who, like the Jews, had been imprisoned because of their race, labelled as *untermenschen*, or 'subhuman'. Later, he had had another clash with the camp administration and had been put on punishment rations. This time the Chinese had returned the favour and saved him by sharing their food. Eventually, his father had tracked down an official linked to the camp who was prepared to take a bribe, and through this he had managed to get Kees returned home to The Hague. After that, Kees had contacted Jan Boone, his school-time friend and Truida's fiancé, for help. Jan had asked Willem to shelter Kees to avoid the risk of meeting his old contacts still in the *Waffen SS*.

Kees related the story to Kieks with pride. He admitted he had been duped by the Nazi propaganda, but was proud that when he had seen what was really going on, he had had the courage and conviction to fight them. He knew of others who had been equally disturbed by the inhuman Nazi activities, but had stayed and continued to obey their orders, carrying out whatever atrocities they were told to do, just because they were too frightened to resist.

Kieks was stunned, unable to make sense of what he was telling her. The sense of stark betrayal was overwhelming, cutting like a knife through the fabric of her trust. They had promised they would keep no secrets from one another, and then this. She had worked with him, lived with him for these months, even years, taking risks with him on the fine line between living and dying, trusting him with her very life – and had had no idea of this secret, this deception.

She needed to get away from him and gather her thoughts.

Her mind was flooded with memories of the various times they had been near Germans, or had heard of Gestapo raids that had taken out members of their group, and she started wondering if Kees still had links with them. The tension in Doordrecht – was this the real reason the local team had turned on him? The shooting in the churchyard; she hadn't been there – was his story really what had happened? Where did the deception end? Could she become enmeshed in some other event and discover another secret? She found herself confused, wracked with doubt and terrified of having anything more to do with Kees. She had to get away. She left immediately and made her way back to The Hague, desperate to confide in her mother. This time she had no plans to return.

When she got back to Citroenstraat, Kieks' thoughts were in turmoil, and she couldn't make her mind up what to do next. The pictures of Kees in his *Waffen SS* uniform kept flashing into her mind, and she recoiled in horror, repelled by everything the uniform stood for. She tried to reason with herself that she should accept his explanation and that he had been extraordinarily brave to have fought the Nazis from inside the organisation when he had realised he had been duped; but her emotions took over, the revulsion and the fear in equal measure. She had a long talk with her mother, who tried to calm her down. Perhaps it was the built-up tension she had been living under, but she couldn't control her emotions, and her head was spinning, her world unravelling.

Taking stock and determined not to fall apart, she resolved to continue to do what she could for the Resistance effort, despite her thoughts about Kees. She got in touch with her old commander in the local Resistance, letting him know she was back in the area. He knew a bit about her background and her earlier life in the North, and a few days later he came back to discuss a new mission. The betrayals and arrests in the Resistance had been happening all around the country, but at the same time new groups were being set up by new people joining the struggle. He talked of a fighting group up in Leeuwarden, up in North Holland, where she had been brought up. He had heard that a group of brothers had set up a unit there, and he wanted to make contact with them. She had lived in Leeuwarden until she was 14, so she knew the area and had family connections nearby. Would she try to make contact with this group?

When Kieks considered the details of the mission, she thought she might even remember the boys she was being asked to contact from her school days. She decided this would be a good way to prove to herself that she could cope without the help of Kees. This would be an opportunity to keep busy, and after she got back she could think of how to respond to Kees.

So, in mid December 1944, Kieks took her bike and cycled up to the north-east of Holland. It was a journey of some two hundred kilometres, and it took a few days, using a list of addresses she had from the family to find places to stay on her way. She had code phrases to make contact with the brothers, messages to pass on to them, and money to pay for any expenses, but first she had to check out how plausible the whole story was.

Once she arrived at the town, her first step was to visit a distant cousin whom she had visited frequently as a child, a man in his late-fifties called Gustavus and his wife, Christina. Kieks brought greetings from the family in The Hague and was invited to stay and use the guest room. It was a pleasure to stretch out with some space and privacy, something she had missed for a while. As she sat there, she could already feel herself calming down and the confusion ebb away. Her first action was to go into town and search for the three brothers. She eventually tracked them down. One was in hospital recovering from an illness, but the others frequented a local café that she had visited as a youngster.

She casually met them for a first time, talking of renewing their acquaintance, chatting about common friends of those earlier times, and barely hinting at an awareness of the Resistance in the vaguest of ways. The next day she met up with them again, once more talking around the subject, but with perhaps a little more reference to the Resistance. Again probing, but in such a way as to give them a chance to boast of exploits rather than to identify her as a contact. They were vague but relaxed, and this encouraged her; she decided it meant they were not indiscreet, and that they did not think they were being watched.

A third meeting followed soon after, and this time she used one of her code words, but still skirting the subject and implying rather that she was an intermediary and that she had met someone from The Hague who wanted her to make introductions. She told them enough to reassure them that she was someone they could trust, and at the same time she examined their reactions to convince herself that there was no risk of them betraying her. They agreed that when they next met, she would bring along her contact from The Hague. They seemed happy with that and were relaxed as they said goodbye. She arranged to meet them later the next day at the usual corner in town.

The next day, she was at her cousin's house having lunch before going to prepare for the meeting. Gustavus had been working at home, and they chatted about this and that until she went to her room, her mind registering just a little surprise as he followed her in.

All of a sudden, he grabbed her, threw her to the bed and thrust his hand between her legs. She gasped with shock, and then frantically fought back. He was unrelenting, focused intently on one goal, his hand reaching ever further. With a wild struggle she fought hard trying to break his grip and push him off. As she did so, she screamed curses and swore at him at the top of her voice, desperately hoping that someone outside might hear. A stream of every swear word in the Dutch language flew from her mouth, and as she slowly started to succeed in fighting him off, she now screamed a torrent of threats, warning him just what she would do if he ever came near her again; threatening to destroy his marriage, his reputation – in the church, in the town and in the family. As she finally managed to break free, he at last stepped back and stood there with his mouth agape, speechless, stunned at how she had resisted. Trembling with fright and indignation, she grabbed her few possessions from the room and rushed out to where her bike was parked.

She cycled away furiously, focusing only on finding somewhere else to stay. She was shaken by the suddenness of the event and was not sure whom to trust. She had been expecting to fight Germans, not her own relatives. She had several contact names, but they were more distant family members and, at this moment, she didn't want to have anything to do with them. She finally stayed with the first one on her list, but with the memory of Gustavus fresh in her mind, she was uncomfortable about staying more than one night and moved on the next day. The second night, she found a family where she felt it was safe to stay. The farmer and his wife were a couple she remembered from when she had lived locally, who agreed she could stay for a few days.

She was deeply shocked by what had happened. These people were relatives, people she had trusted. She had just left a man who she had trusted until she discovered he been in the *Waffen SS*. Now she had been attacked by someone whom she had thought of as part of her family – another person to be trusted.

It took a couple of days to recover her equilibrium. As she calmed down, she became more concerned about having missed her meeting with the brothers. She felt cross, and wondered how they would react, and what story she would tell them to cover her absence. She cycled back to town and the corner where they had met, and watched out for them. There was no sign of them. She waited patiently for quite a while, but they seemed to have disappeared. After a couple of days, she discreetly asked neighbours, playing on the fact that she used to live here and was back visiting old friends. Everyone seemed nervous and there was no news forthcoming. Eventually, she went back to the hospital, making contact with the third brother. She repeated her story of being from the area and renewing acquaintances. He thought he could remember her from when she had lived there, and eventually opened up.

He told her the Gestapo had arrested the two brothers. The brothers had been the bait at the centre of a trap and the Gestapo had been looking for a third person, a courier from a Resistance group in The Hague. He explained that a meeting had been arranged but the person had not turned up, and the brothers had had no idea why not. The Gestapo had turned on them and had taken them for interrogation. The first brother had been shot and the second brother had died during interrogation. As far as the third brother knew, the Gestapo had not caught the courier.

Kieks absorbed this revelation, concentrating on keeping any trace of alarm from her expression, then quietly paid her condolences and said goodbye, still hiding the emotions that were racing through her mind. She walked outside, climbed on her bike, and set off out of town as quickly as she could, back down the quiet country roads, out to the safety of the farm she had found, as far away as possible from any Gestapo.

As she cycled, all she could think about was that she was only alive because Gustavus had tried to rape her. He was an animal, a beast, but if he had not attacked her, she would be as dead as the two brothers. It was wrong, it was unbelievable, but it meant she had survived.

She didn't dwell too long on what had happened, but knew it was time to head home. She still had her stash of money and she now focused on visiting neighbouring farms and steadily buying food to bring back to The Hague. One of her early stops was at Twello, where Ruurd had moved to after the Allies had advanced to Arnhem. He gave her a large cake of salt, a rare commodity now, as civilians were not allowed down to the shore because of the defences against invasion. She wrapped it up and sent it to her family, putting it on a barge which was travelling down to The Hague. Afterwards she learnt that, a few days later, the barge had been bombed and her parcel was gone.

She stayed a few more days at another farm and, after a week or so, set off home, taking further diversions to do some more foraging as she made her way back. Home lay almost on the other side of the country and food was far more plentiful here, away from the big towns. It was a cold, grey day, with a dusting of snow covering the fields and occasional flakes blowing into her face. The roads were deserted and there was not a sound to be heard.

As she cycled, her mind drifted back to the events in Leeuwarden. Gustavus: she had seen absolutely no warning signs that he might jump on her – but at least she had been able to fight him off. And the brothers: there had been no warning signs there either; she thought she had learnt to spot the signs of treachery from her time with Kees, but even so, thinking back, there had been no signs of a trap. And the only reason she had escaped capture was because Gustavus had attacked her. Surely that wasn't how God would look after her?

Her thoughts also drifted to Kees. As she looked back over the recent events, she realised now how much he had protected her while they had worked together in Haarlemmermeer. The way events had unfolded emphasised how unpredictable the future was. Kees hadn't known what the *Waffen SS* would evolve into when he had joined it, but he had done something about it when he had realised what it was; he had been courageous to fight it from the inside, and to have made his break. He had been right, it had been a brave thing to do, and she had judged him too harshly. She would have to go back and try to rebuild the relationship.

She was confused and troubled, but as she cycled she became aware of the silence and the tranquillity that surrounded her. Only the squeaks and rattles of the bike were to be heard. For a brief moment in this war, she could relax and allow her mind to wander and reflect.

As she rounded a bend, she abruptly came across a convoy of what looked like three large farm trailers forming a blockage in the middle of the road. The wagons were covered with tarpaulins and there were a number of country folk sitting on them. At first glance all seemed rather ordinary, but at the same time something seemed strange and out of place, and she couldn't put her finger on it. Then, as the tarpaulins flapped in the wind, she caught a glimpse of the outline of a large metal frame with several round holes, and strange fins sticking out of the sides. She immediately felt a pang of fear: these were not agricultural trailers.

As she scanned the scene in front of her, some German soldiers appeared out of nowhere and told her to get off her bike. She realised that she had stumbled across some kind of secret Nazi convoy. It must be one of Hitler's secret weapons that she had heard about in the BBC broadcasts; possibly a V1 launching system – the 'doodlebug', a pilotless aircraft fitted with a large bomb. Possibly it was a V2 rocket; she couldn't see under the tarpaulin so she couldn't be sure. Whatever it was, she knew from reports on the BBC that these unmanned flying missiles were being fired at South East England and terror-bombing London, and as far as she had heard, nobody knew where they were being fired from.

One of the guards told her to get off her bike and join the group of other locals who, like her, had stumbled across the convoy. It appeared that one truck had broken down, and after a short while and a few more passers-by had been rounded up, they were grouped together and ordered to help push it into the neighbouring field. With a struggle, they pushed it off the road and a few metres away from the edge and into the field. They were then ordered to get back onto the trailer and sit there. A guard told them that they would have to wait until dark when the Gestapo would arrive to deal with them, and she was ordered to sit with the others on one of the carts. As she looked around, she realised that the civilians provided useful camouflage to fool the surveillance planes that occasionally appeared in the sky.

As the significance of what she had stumbled on sank in, she started to shake; convinced she was going to die. At first, remembering that her description had been circulated round the Gestapo, she began to panic that she might be recognised. As the seriousness of the situation sank in, she took stock of the way that the Gestapo worked. A creeping conviction came over her that everyone here who had seen this would be killed, just to protect the secret mission. She also thought of the events in Leeuwarden; after surviving all that, she was going to be shot just for being in the wrong place at the wrong time. She was petrified. According to Gestapo routine, either she would be interrogated and tortured into telling them all about the Jews in the house, or else she and everyone around her would be shot out of hand. Either way meant certain death.

Weighing up what was happening around her, Kieks made a calculated decision, and set her mind on a course of action. Spontaneously, the memories of her struggle with Gustavus seemed to have planted a seed in her mind. As she looked around, she realised that all the other hostages were men; perhaps she had a weapon that they didn't have, her own secret weapon. At that particular moment, the guards had little to do; they were killing time as they waited for night to fall. She thought back to the brief encounter with the guard who had intercepted her. He had not been unpleasant, just business-like, and he was not much older than she was. With no clear plan, and not quite knowing what might happen next, she summoned up all her courage and called out to him. With a seductiveness that belied the terror inside her, she quietly and sweetly suggested that he take her behind one of the wagons, out of sight of the prisoners and the other guards, where they could be together in private. He was surprised, but happy to oblige.

Drawing on all her feminine wiles for survival, she fulfilled her part of the bargain, and afterwards she persuaded him to leave her lying there on the ground. For a few seconds she could gather herself and think of trying to escape.

The ground was covered with a light layer of snow, and in the grey overcast light, the landscape was bleak and featureless. She could see that she was not too far from a slight depression at the foot of a hedge – several yards distant. To run for it would be to run across open ground in sight of the other Germans. If they saw her run, they would shoot first and ask questions later. If she moved slowly it might be safer: perhaps if they did see her they might call her back, instead of shooting her.

Terror gripped her to her core, but she knew this might be her only chance. Slowly, slowly she started to roll herself towards the hedge. At each turn, she froze stock-still and held her breath, expecting the shouts or bullets from a German guard. As she rolled, the snow caked onto her coat and she hoped that she was perhaps building up a white layer that might help her blend into the surroundings. She continued her excruciatingly slow journey, now rolling across the open ground in plain sight of the guards, pausing at every sound she made in the snow. Every move she made was inch-by-inch, as slowly, as quietly as possible, but she was now in full view of them, and they had nothing to do but look in her direction – and yet she seemed to be invisible to the guards even when they were looking straight at her. Eventually, she edged her way into the depression, but realised she was still in their line of sight. As she lay there, one stood up and started walking towards her. She froze for an interminable moment, watching his silhouette looming towards her outlined against the grey sky, stifling her breath and trying to keep as still as possible, terrified at what would happen next.

A short distance from her, he stopped. The only thought in her mind was *please don't shoot me, please don't shoot me*. He paused and then turned back to the others. She lay there, unable to think, unable to turn her head to watch them except from the corner of her eye. She lay there, petrified, convinced that at any moment she would be spotted and shot. She didn't move, just lay there staring up at the sky, possibly for hours, completely unable to see what was happening around her and unaware of the time. Eventually, she drifted into a numbing trance, thinking only of the guard who might come back again at any time.

With time, darkness fell, but she barely sensed it, remaining where she was, paralysed, rigid with fear, expecting at every moment a guard to walk back over, but this time to spot her and shoot.

Suddenly, gunfire and screams cracked through the darkness. The clamour sheared through her trance and she stiffened, listening intently, waiting for her turn, wondering if she had been spotted. The gunfire continued after the screams had died away, and then it too stopped. There was a silence for some minutes, and then she heard a car drive away. She knew then they had left her on her own, unseen. She was now completely on her own. And she had been right. Death had been waiting for her, but she had escaped. All the other people she had been with in the field must now be dead. Their bodies would be out there, scattered in the snow.

She waited, listening a while longer, then carefully picked herself up in the darkness. She didn't want to risk stumbling over the bodies in the dark, so she made her way to the road, skirting the area where the wagons had been. She scrabbled around in the dark looking for where she had put down her bike. The bike was still in the hedge where she had left it, and in a state of numbed shock, eventually she managed to make her way back to where she had been staying. She said nothing to her hosts and went straight to bed.

Her mind was numb. The events seemed to belong to another world. They couldn't have happened to her. They were too awful. Her mind refused to think about or make sense of what had happened; it was too traumatic, too incomprehensible.

In spite of the shattering experience, for the days that followed, she continued her foraging, almost on automatic pilot, focusing on gathering food to avoid thinking of what had happened, and in early January she was ready to go home to Citroenstraat and her family. Her last contact gave her an extra treat of a few pancakes and four cigars 'to bribe the guards on the way home'. When she saw the cigars, she swore to herself that the Germans would not get them. She crammed her provisions into two bags and covered the top of one with a bag of grain and the other with beans.

She watched out carefully as she cycled along, concentrating on the road and surroundings to avoid thinking of the devastating event. For most of her journey she was able to bypass roadblocks, but she knew there were two she could not avoid. Her route took her along one of the dykes that protected Holland's shore, and there were guards at either end. As she arrived at the first checkpoint, she came up behind an ammunition truck which had just had its papers checked and was pulling away. In a moment of recklessness, she grabbed hold of the fender at the back, and was whisked forward past the startled guard. He raised his gun and pointed it at her, calling for her to come back, but he didn't dare to shoot at the loaded truck, and the driver didn't seem to hear him. She guessed that he wouldn't dare to report it either; he would be punished if he admitted letting her get through.

She soon let go of the fender and continued cycling until she got to the other end, but here she had to face the guards. Her bags contained butter, cheese and a variety of scarce fresh vegetables such as cauliflower, chicory and carrots. She knew they would help themselves to anything they fancied, so when they asked her what was in the bags, she promptly said, 'Ten kilograms of wheat and eight kilograms of beans'. These were of little interest to them, and as a further distraction, she pulled out a couple of the pancakes from a pocket and offered them to the guards. They were pleased with this little treat and waved her through without further ado.

She made her way on to a cousin's house that lay on the way to The Hague, and offered him the cigars as a possibility for trade. He was delighted with them and swapped them for a 22kg bag of wheat to take back home. She got back on the bike, with the bag of wheat balanced on the handlebars. The bike was now very unstable as the loose grain in the sack flowed from side to side, and it was a slow journey as she wobbled her way back home.

When she finally arrived home, it was five minutes before the eight o'clock curfew and the family helped her indoors. As she arrived her period started, and when she realised this, she breathed a sigh of relief and hoped that this marked a point where she could put the whole ordeal of what had happened behind her. It was the 12th of January 1945, her 23rd birthday, and she had been away for two days short of a month.

For a couple of days, she sat at home talking with Moeder, trying to make sense of what had happened, but some things were too distressing for her to speak out loud. Regardless of wanting to forget the dreadful events, a small voice inside her head told her she wasn't finished; she had yet more to do. She was convinced that the news of the secret weapons and the massacre she had witnessed in the field needed to be reported to London as soon as possible. Within days she made her way to a man she knew who could pass on messages to London. She told him her story, and as she described the key parts of the horrifying events in that field, she found herself shaking uncontrollably. The man was incredulous, but assured her that the news would be passed on.

Once she had made her report, she returned home to rest and to try to sort out in her mind what had happened. She tried to talk about it with Moeder, but found it difficult: she couldn't bring herself to talk about Gustavus, and she could hardly talk about the German soldier. There was such a mix of emotions and shame as she tried to explain what had happened, that she couldn't properly express herself or reveal the nature of her shame, so her mother could not fully grasp what had happened, only that she was deeply traumatised by the events. The thought of contacting the Resistance commander did not cross Kieks' mind. She knew that with the events of the last few days everything had changed, and she needed time to get over the events, time to make sense of it all.

In The Hague, the famine was gradually getting worse. The retaliation for the Dutch railway strike was still in place, the Germans had cut off all food and fuel shipments into the western provinces and were still preventing all foodstuffs from coming into the city. There was no food to be had anywhere. Anything that could be eaten had already gone, and any morsels left were being used as bait to try to catch whatever living creatures were around. The family cat was gone, its skin spotted in a nearby garden, and even mice and rats were being eaten. Kieks' supply of food could not last long when it was shared among the fourteen in the house, which now included Trijntje, Dirk and their new baby, Miente[39].

For a few days, Kieks tried to recover from her shattering ordeal. It was not easy because space was limited: the house was now almost full to bursting with people coming and going. In addition to the original seven family members, there were now three spouses (Jan

---

[39] Pronunciation: Miente = _Meen_-tuh.

Boone, Dirk Bakker and Diny Okma), the five Jews, as well as occasional visitors. Those people who did come for a social visit thought that the Okma household was relatively safe, well away from any Resistance work or any Jews in hiding.

After a few days spent struggling with her turbulent feelings, Kieks again talked with her mother, eventually shamefully, desperately pouring out everything that had happened. Moeder was stunned but was not judgemental and consoled her that God would not condemn her. She also urged Kieks to move away again, reminding her that she had been on a Gestapo wanted list – although Moeder might also have been trying to get Kieks away from the crowd and stress in the household. The next day Kieks went off to her cousins, Wil and Wim Spaans, who lived nearby.

Kieks' move took her away from the house, but she was now quite close and she regularly visited the family home. She tried to rationalise what had happened to her and compare it with what Kees had done. Somehow it now seemed much easier to understand his choices; after all, what she had done could also be described in very damning ways, just as bad as his act of joining the *Waffen*

SS. But she found she couldn't dwell on her own experiences for too long, or her head started spinning in turmoil.

She could also see how much Kees had protected her from the worst of the dangers, and how terribly brave he had been in fighting the *Waffen SS* from the inside. The more she thought of Kees, the more awful she felt. How could she face him? When he had been threatened by the *Waffen SS*, he had fought them from the inside and then fled; when she had faced the danger of the Germans in the field, she had seduced a soldier and then fled. And she couldn't keep it secret from him; they had promised not to keep secrets from each other, and in any case, he would know there was something wrong; this secret was eating her up from the inside. But she couldn't face him yet; she needed time to reflect and to find a way to reclaim herself-respect. So for now, she made no attempt to make contact with Kees.

She missed being close to her mother, and when she was at the house, Piet would take her aside and tell her how much Moeder missed her and wanted her around. But when she spoke to her mother, the message was different: Moeder was still terrified that the Gestapo would come looking for her, and so she wanted Kieks to stay safely away. She also assured Kieks that the other family members were now each taking their turn going out to look for food and bringing in supplies, and she needn't worry about helping.

The shortages went beyond food; there was virtually no power or fuel, and the house was cold and dark. A few people had managed to tap into priority German power cables but the Okmas were not among them. In the evening, they had to do everything around the house in the dark or occasionally with candles.

Smoking helped ease the hunger pains and everyone took it up. Tobacco was almost impossible to find, but a number of plants were being used as substitutes. Cigarette paper was also in short supply. Kieks had been given a fine pocket Bible in her teenage years and through all her adversities she had remained strongly religious, sustained by a gently comforting feeling that God was looking after her. Now she finally weakened, and tore out sheets of the fine paper to use for rolling cigarettes. Over the past years she had often turned to it for spiritual comfort, but soon her Bible shrank until only her favourite passages were left.

On her visits home to Citroenstraat, Kieks again was aware of the tension filling the air. The Jewish *onderduikers* seemed to know parts of the story about Kees and his time in the *Waffen SS,* although she didn't know how the news had filtered back to the people in the house. The Jews seemed particularly frightened by the story, and Kieks convinced herself they were angry with her because she had been his girlfriend and supporter in the house. She felt they were scrutinising her every time they talked about him, as if she had known full well that he was in the SS when he had first arrived. It made her think again about what he had done and how she had judged him. Once more she reflected on how difficult it must have been for him to change from being a *Waffen SS* officer to a Resistance fighter. Of course, when talking to the refugees in the house, she stopped herself from ever defending him, because that would have revealed what the two of them had been doing for the last six months; and so she held her silence as they voiced their fears.

Piercing hunger persisted through the *Hongerwinter*, and the daily hunt for food continued, the family members all foraging in their own way. Willem managed to acquire a large load of sugar beet, which was unloaded and stored in one of the bedrooms. Sugar beet has a very sickly sweet taste and isn't used in normal cooking, but these were desperate times and it was almost the only thing they could find to eat. They cooked it in a stew, adding carrots, greens and tulip bulbs. The tulip bulbs had a very bitter taste, which cut through the sickly taste of the sugar beet and made the stew at least partly edible. However, as the centre of the bulb is poisonous, they had to be used sparingly. The household's choice was limited: either the incessant hunger pains, or the slightly less painful stomach cramps from the toxins in the bulbs. This stew was virtually the only staple food the people in Citroenstraat had to eat in the final months of the war, and they all recognised that it was probably the only thing keeping them from starving to death.

It was a bitterly cold winter, and in the local churches, bodies were gathering as the starving undertakers no longer had the strength to dig graves in the frozen ground. As Kieks walked the streets in those days, she could see how the famine was affecting other people. Everywhere she looked she saw people with swollen wrist and ankle joints, lumbering in slow motion, symptoms of the chronic starvation that so many were suffering. As she looked around, she found some comfort in telling herself that at least no one in their house was suffering from these symptoms.

Kieks was still staying with the Spaans, and would cycle out into the countryside to find provisions, frequently visiting home with a bag of more varied groceries to swap for some of the sugar beet. She would take several beets in return for a loaf of bread and some butter. During these exchanges, she was often aware of carping comments from the others, in particular her sister, Ella, who felt that the trade was unbalanced.

Some of the food she took to the local black market, and here she used it to gather the guilders needed to pay for Jantje's keep, for which she was still taking full responsibility. When Ella found her out on one occasion, they had a blazing row. Ella shouted that she was betraying the family, selling the food they desperately needed to raise money for her own petty luxuries. Kieks defended herself, explaining how she was raising money for Jantje, but, because she refused to give details, her sister dismissed her story, not believing a word. After all she had gone through, and now to have her family start picking on her, she found the unresolved memories of her trip to Leeuwarden started to come streaming back, crowding in on her, challenging her ability to cope, and Kieks found herself becoming more and more snappy and sullen.

Martha was still principal at the crèche, and one child there had now starved to the point that he was simply lying motionless all day. She told Kieks about him, who found herself trying to think of a plan: having something to focus on helped take her mind off things. After their talk, Martha brought the starving 3-year-old Davy to the house. Kieks balanced the torpid child on the seat on the back of her bike and set off to find him somewhere to stay out in the country, where there was more food to be had.

As soon as she left the house she was cycling through an area where five-floor apartment blocks lined wide streets. The Germans had parked weapon systems in many of the streets, possibly in the hope that the Allies would avoid bombing so close to civilians. However, the Allies were not deterred and as she arrived, an air-raid started. As the American planes came close, Kieks rushed with Davy to a shelter.

Eventually the raid was over and they could emerge. In front of them, the wooden structure of a large church burned fiercely, and all around flames leapt to the sky, reaching up from the houses and sometimes joining those rising from the other side of the street. All that could be heard was the roar of the flames.

Kieks looked round. The street was strewn with body after body dressed in prison fatigues, shot dead, wearing signs stating 'Looter'. She looked round in horror, then grabbed Davy and set off on her bike towards the countryside.

Later she was to discover that a local prison had caught fire in a previous raid that day, and that the Governor had released the men, under the pretext that their records had been destroyed and they now had a unique opportunity to start again. Around eighty men had been released, and forty-five had been shot as looters before the day was out.

Kieks cycled on until she reached the village of Badhoevedorp, where she had a Resistance contact. The family offered to look after the child, but after they had talked a while, Kieks decided against it. Three of the household had been shot recently for possessing guns and she felt the Gestapo might come back. Instead, she cycled out to someone whom she knew to be a friend of her sister, Truida, and arranged to leave the child there. Making contact took only fifteen minutes and, almost immediately, Kieks had left.

As news came of Allied forces advancing further into Holland and liberating the eastern and northern provinces, the Germans tightened their grip on the western provinces. Kieks found she could no longer contribute much to the Resistance, but not only because of her state of mind: the organisation was in tatters and there were no more operations. Instead, she was limited to regularly visiting three families who were sheltering Jews, bringing them a few meagre rations and a little money. There was so little food around that she couldn't make much of a contribution, and she felt that her greatest help was in giving them reassurance that they were not alone. 'Sit tight, it won't be long now.'

In Willemsdorp, Jantje had become registered as the natural child of his foster mother, Jantje, so the risk of him being identified as a Jew had disappeared. In early 1945, their house was on the front line, with the Allied forces camped on the other side of the river from where the house stood. The Germans had ordered the evacuation of the family, and Jantje, the mother, had left her hut and taken her two children to a local school where they remained for some time. Throughout this they were treated as a normal family unit. Kieks had not been able to visit them for the past two months but was pleased that the child's cover was now completely secure. She decided it was best to keep it that way, so still didn't pass the information on to the local Resistance. The memory of Kees fending off probing questions about Jantje was still on her mind, and the fear of betrayal was too strong for her to take the risk.

Piet and Lien saw this security as a double-edged sword and worried that perhaps the foster mother would become too attached to the child and try to hold on to him after the war. As far as they knew, there was no one apart from Kieks, the Okmas and the foster mother who knew the child was theirs. Kieks found she didn't have the energy to reassure them. She told them Jantje was with an honest family and they just had to trust them. She just wanted it all to stop.

As the Allies restarted their offensive, the Dutch population became more excited at the prospects of liberation. The German forces recognised they were facing defeat, and there were reports that in some quarters, Jews had come out of hiding and were being left unmolested. Snippets were reported on the BBC and so everyone in the house was aware of developments. Nonetheless, Willem was suspicious and eventually decided that the reports may be true, but that the people who had hidden them might have been arrested and taken away. Moeder was particularly worried and told the younger Okmas that they were not to let the Jews in the house know what was happening. They also made plans that if the Jews did hear the news and go out, then Kieks and Willem would go into hiding.

Finally, after the Germans negotiated their surrender, the war ended on the 5th May. However, for a couple of days the German forces in Amsterdam were free to hold onto their weapons, waiting until the Canadian forces entered the city to disarm and intern them. News spread that the Canadians were only a few miles away. The Dutch populace flocked excitedly to Dam Square, in the heart of the city centre, *'De Dam'*. Among them were

Trijntje's brother-in-law, Popke, and his wife. A jubilant chant started from the crowd –'*Canada! Canada!*'– as the various German soldiers looked on, with increasing frustration. For one soldier, this was too much to bear. He grasped a machine gun and started firing on the crowd. Everyone dived for cover, and Popke threw himself over his wife to protect her. In seconds, over twenty people lay bleeding and dying. Popke died the next day.

When the liberation was announced, Piet and the others could come out of hiding and breathe freely at last. They had escaped their certain death in the shelter of the Okma house. Chris moved out immediately, crossing over the road back to where he had been staying before the Gestapo raid. The other Jews stayed for a few days until they found a place to move to, and then quickly moved on. Kieks returned to Citroenstraat on the 30th May, twenty-five days after the end of the war. By the time she returned, all the refugees had left and the house was once again the family home.

Kieks reflected on the time they had spent in the house. The *onderduikers* had all entered the Okmas' house for what was anticipated to be a few months but had turned out to be an interminable stay of almost three years. They had all survived this abominable war, and none of them suffered the swollen joints and other signs of starvation that were so prominent with many Dutch people on the streets. There had been eleven people sharing a small house, rising to fifteen near the end. As food had become increasingly scarce, the tensions between them had often come close to breaking point. They had been strangers, from very different backgrounds, cultures and lifestyles, brought together by the war and forced to live in each other's presence for nearly three years. When it was all finished, there was no sense of jubilation, no sense of camaraderie or gratitude, only a deep relief that it was all over and a determination to put it behind them, go their separate ways and start rebuilding their lives as quickly as possible.

Kieks now met up with Captain Herman, her shadowy controller in the local Resistance. He gave her a uniform and helmet, telling her the returned Dutch government was now issuing Resistance workers with military uniforms, giving recognition to their role in working for the Resistance. She was briefly able to walk round in her khaki and helmet, meeting two other women who had had similar experiences to her own, and posing for a photo. She wore the uniform for one last task. Davy, the young child whom she had moved in the last months of the war, was now fully recovered and becoming an unmanageable handful for his foster parents. As a city child in the country he was out of place, and his foster parents phoned the Okmas and asked for him to be brought back to his family. Kieks donned her uniform, collected him and brought him to his parents, her last job in the Resistance. When she returned home, Truida was there to take her to task, indignant at the way in which Kieks had imposed on her friends. Kieks was too tired to discuss it and made no apology for her actions.

Kieks (left), Capt. Herman and two Resistance workers (Barrie and Jopie[40]) in the uniforms given to them by Commandant Herman, in The Hague, May 1945

Towards the end and immediately after the war, Kieks was to hear reports of the Dutch authorities finding mysterious groups of perhaps thirty-or-so civilians slaughtered in various fields in northern Holland, apparently shot for no obvious reason. When she heard about them, she was convinced that these were groups of people who had stumbled across the V1 or V2 convoys, as she had. One of these groups must have been the one

---

[40] Pronunciation: Barrie = *Bah-ree*; Jopie = *Yoh-pee*.

where she had so narrowly escaped from being another of the bodies in the snow.

The Dutch people had suffered as much hardship at the hands of the Nazis as any of the other occupied territories in Western Europe, and as they began to recover their freedom, they were also coping with the profound effects the war had had on their collective psyche. For Kieks, the emotional scars she bore were still fresh and vivid, but with the war now over, she had to put them behind her and start a new chapter. There was no help to uncover and heal the wounds, and they were to be with her for a long time to come.

Part 2

Once the war had ended, the Dutch government set up investigatory panels looking into everything from possible war crimes to minor instances of anti-Semitism. A few months on, a letter arrived for Willem, the first official acknowledgement of his role in protecting the Jews. It was from one of the minor panels, which told him that a complaint had been received and a decision had been made to investigate a report of anti-Semitism. The report was that Willem had been abusing and insulting Jews. He was called to face the panel and answer the charges.

As the enquiry unfolded, it soon became clear that it was all connected with the incident when he had spotted Joop leaning out of the window in full view of the street, and the angry language that he had used in reaction. When Willem was called to testify, he described the circumstances and repeated the words he had used: 'Keep your face away from the bedroom window! Your big Jewish nose will be spotted and we will all be taken by the Gestapo!' His story was unchallenged and the case was dismissed. The tribunal chairman, himself Jewish, privately offered his sympathies to Willem: 'What you and your family did was good work. This should never have been brought in front of the panel'.

The event deeply upset the family in light of the hardships all of them, including the Jewish *onderduikers*, had endured. Kieks especially, having at times experienced the brunt of Joop's abrasiveness, felt angry, indignant and insulted.

Having spent the war confined in the Okmas' house it was perhaps not unsurprising that Joop lashed out at the people who had both been his protectors and his jailors. His whole world had been reduced to the events in the Okma house and in the room behind the mirror. And so the incident with Willem was one of the very few events where there was real action and it had festered in his mind as a major injustice. Perhaps Joop felt this tribunal was the only way he could receive official recognition of his suffering. The Jews in the house suffered in quite a different way to the Okmas.

With the war over, Piet could now reclaim his true name, Sallie. He and his wife, Lien, quickly went to collect their son, whom they could now speak of as Bram instead of as Jantje. They followed Kieks' directions and travelled to Willemsdorp, where they found the house set between the dyke and the water, surrounded by traces of the few pigs that had lived there till recently. Kieks had told them that Bram was now formally registered as Jantje, the son of the woman Jantje, and his new status troubled Sallie and Lien. All sorts of scenarios may have played out in their minds as they prepared to collect him. Many young children had disappeared, possibly adopted, and would they ever get him back?

When they reached the house between the dykes, they found an elderly man, and their first thought was probably that he had papers to show that he was the child's grandfather. Sallie introduced himself and his wife and told the old man that young Jantje was Bram, his son, and that he wanted to see him immediately. The child was produced without hesitation and Grandfather tried to invite them in, but Sallie declined. He was distressed by the overwhelming sense of poverty that clung to the shack, and the aroma of the unclean pigs was an unpleasant reminder that his son had been staying in an environment which was entirely abhorrent to his religion. After a few hurried words, he turned with his wife and son, and set off for their new life.

The poor foster family were still owed the money for the last two months and Kieks visited a few weeks later to settle the outstanding debt and to say thank you. Kieks felt an overwhelming wave of anger towards Sallie for the lack of gratitude and callous sudden removal of the child, but at the same time, wondered if she was overreacting and letting her emotions get out of control.

The Hekschers soon got over the shock of the poverty and the pigs at Willemsdorp, and without prompting, quickly went back to say their own profound thank you. In later years they made several visits, and Bram was to spend several summer holidays at the farm – even though they were farming pigs – maintaining the bond of affection that had formed in these early years.

Sallie and his family returned to their home village of Coevorden, near the German border. Most of their relatives and friends had been wiped out in the Holocaust. He and his wife had had fourteen brothers and sisters between them before the war, now only one survived. The local synagogue had had a congregation of several thousand before the war, but afterwards perhaps only forty returned.

Fortunately for Sallie, his lawyer had continued to manage his affairs meticulously throughout the war, and the man had been pleased and proud to hand back to

Sallie all the deeds to his properties. It was then that Sallie was reminded of the visit to Citroenstraat in 1942 by the man with the red stripe on his trousers, and discovered the explanation for the mysterious visit.

The man had in fact been a private investigator. The conscientious lawyer had been keeping Sallie's drapery business running profitably, putting the profits to one side until the moment he would be able to return them to their owner. The man who had first brought Sallie into contact with the Okmas went by the name of Kraantje, and he had realised that the lawyer had access to Sallie's money, and so had tried to get his hands on some of it. He had told the lawyer that Sallie was being looked after by the Okmas and they needed money to buy provisions, claiming that he had been asked to get funds and pass them on. The careful lawyer hired the investigator to go into the house and listen for the sounds of other people living upstairs. The report eventually came back that there were no signs of refugees living there, and with that, the lawyer had refused to hand over anything. There was also a suggestion that when he didn't get any money, Kraantje had tried to spread rumours about where the Hekschers might be hiding. Fortunately, no one had paid any attention to him.

The Heckshers soon renewed contact with the Okmas and the two families maintained good and friendly relations for many years.

The strains of living on top of each other for three years had left their toll, and for a while, little was said between the younger Okmas and the refugees as they went their separate ways. Kieks felt that her family had given everything to people who had continually taken but never given, while the refugees, who knew nothing of the daily hardships the family had endured beyond their hiding place, felt they had been prisoners as much as guests, and had found it stressful having no control of their lives and having to rely on strangers for their every need; living a life which was alien to everything they had experienced before the war.

Kieks slowly adjusted to life without the refugees. There was a sense of victory in having beaten the Nazis by successfully sheltering the *onderduikers*, but the sense of loss was much greater: the loss of friends and family over the last years, the disruption of their close family bonds, and the unsettling way the Jews had departed with so little acknowledgement after so much effort to keep them alive. Their dangerous work risking their lives for the Resistance also seemed to be disregarded; the Dutch government did little to support the former Resistance workers at this time, as it concentrated its efforts on the overwhelmingly massive task of rebuilding the country after the ravages of war. In the immediate years after the war, Kieks felt it was as if their contribution had been judged pointless and irrelevant. At times she felt despondently flat, at other times she was just angry.

Chris was reunited with his children very soon after the war ended. Martha had visited them regularly and had brought him news of how they were doing, so that was one worry he had not had to face. There had been tensions between Chris and the others in the house, and after they went their separate ways, the Van Gelderens and the Hekschers broke all contact with him. However, Martha remained very close to Chris and to his daughter Lisette, and she and Chris even considered marriage, although the religious differences proved too insurmountable for both of them. In later years, Chris's eldest daughter, Lisette, was to spend some summer holidays together with members of the Okma family.

The Van Gelderens – Joop and Bep – had a more tortuous journey to reunite their family. They had put their two young children into hiding in 1942, but when the war ended they had no idea where their children were or even whether they had survived the war. For a long time they worked tirelessly trying to track them down, contacting all the various tracking agencies, including Jewish foundations, police authorities, organisations such as the Red Cross, and a government agency set up to track people who had been in hiding. At first they found a number of more distant family members who had survived their own ordeals, but there was no sign of their own children.

Their eldest was Carrie, who had been sheltered by the family of Piet Brakel's brother, Jet and Wim, until Piet was captured and tortured. The family had moved her as soon as Piet Brakel had been detained, transferring her to Friesland where she had been looked after by a second set of foster parents. These foster parents and Carrie had grown very fond of each other and the family found it hard to hand her over. Eventually the families made contact and Carrie had been handed back to Joop and Bep, an event Carrie herself found quite traumatic.

Their other child was Ernst, who had been sheltered by another church member, and by coincidence had been living in a home in Abrikozenstraat, a street running directly behind Citroenstraat. He had been picked up in a Gestapo raid immediately after the torturing of Piet Brakel and had been sitting locked in the van parked outside number 18 while the Gestapo team had gone on to raid the Okma household. He was later taken to Scheveningen Prison, and subsequently put on a train to a concentration camp. By an amazing stroke of sheer good luck, he was saved by someone from the Resistance, plucked from the train[41] by an individual determined to deprive the Nazis of at least one victim. He was then put in the hands of a second set of foster parents, and finally returned to his parents a year after the end of the war. Joop, Bep and their reunited family kept in touch with Martha for several years, and continued their friendship with the Hekschers for the rest of their lives.

---

[41] The records show him listed as getting on the train but not present on the disembarkation list.

Ruurd and his wife Corrie had managed to sustain their young family through the war. Despite the war, Ruurd's business had prospered, and he had bought a paint factory in a nearby town. Some three years after he had bought it, a fire had razed it to the ground. There had been a large quantity of sulphur stored in the factory and when it had caught fire, the toxic fumes had drifted over the town, which then had to be evacuated. This storage had been a breach in the regulations and Ruurd had been heavily fined, losing most of what he had made during the war.

Douwe returned to normal life and, as far as Kieks could see, he adjusted with little difficulty. On occasions, he mused that when he wanted to travel somewhere by train, his first urge was sometimes to print himself a ticket – before reminding himself that this was no longer appropriate. He and Tiny had one child, Dirk, who was born in 1943.

Ella had taught throughout the war, though she had often been ill. After the war, the doctors spotted a shadow on her lungs, which they had said may have been a mild form of tuberculosis, and she had to stop teaching until this eventually faded away. Then she could continue her teaching career. She had become closely involved in the work of sheltering the Jews in the year after Kieks had left and was very proud of what the family had done. In the years following the war, she vigorously supported the Zionist movement and was inspired by its efforts to form a Jewish homeland in Palestine. She also became an enthusiastic ambassador for Esperanto, the newly invented language, which its proponents believed could replace the multitude of languages and lead to understanding and peace across the world. She travelled round Europe attending Esperanto conferences until the early 1970s.

After their marriage, Trijntje and Dirk had moved to the city of Groningen in the north-east of Holland. In the autumn of 1944, they had gone into hiding to avoid the forced labour squads and had ended up back in Citroenstraat, where they had stayed until the end of the war. Then they had to deal with the fallout from the death of Dirk's brother, Popke, who had been killed when the German soldier had fired on the crowd in Dam Square, two days after the end of the war. Instead of returning to Groningen, they moved to Amsterdam, where Dirk took charge of the firm that had belonged to Popke.

Martha left the house in 1945 and moved a short distance away. Jan and Truida married in 1945 and moved out to the nearby street of Galileistraat, and then in 1952, moved on to another house in Leeuweriklaan, where Ella and Moeder joined them.

The last of the Okmas to leave Citroenstraat were Willem and Diny, who left in 1953 and moved to Apeldoorn in central Holland.

Some of the Okmas leaving Citroenstraat after the war

The relationship between Kieks and Kees had ended abruptly when she had discovered the *Waffen SS* link. Her own harrowing experience had brought home to Kieks what an achievement it had been for Kees to escape the clutches of the *Waffen SS*; she now recognised the bravery and courage in his actions, and the heroic way he had protected her. Eventually she took her own courage in hand and made contact with Kees, steeling herself to tell the story of the events in the field. But Kees had news of his own to give her. He had decided he was too young and the future too uncertain to be committed to one girl, to be engaged. After her sudden departure, he had moved on with his life and had made new friendships with a couple of girls. He wanted the freedom to explore this new lifestyle. He told Kieks that he wanted to end to their engagement. They should continue to go their separate ways. Kieks felt numb and returned home in a daze, her hopes shattered.

Reeling from another knock, Kieks found it hard to adjust to the new peace and the mundane routines of ordinary life. During the war there had been continual stress, fear and tension, but the time had also been infused with extraordinary excitement and adventure, a feeling that others depended on her, and that she was doing something important. That was all gone.

Some of the memories from the war were happy ones. Thinking of the mischievous operations in the tulip fields always made her feel good, and she embroidered a small scene as a reminder of the occasion when she had helped remove fuel from right under the gaze of the Germans. For many years she kept the picture on her wall, of a tulip field with a small punt in the foreground and a tulip barn in the background.

It was now time to plan for the future, and Kieks thought back to the rescue at Hoofddorp, where she had helped the wounded Resistance fighters. She decided to train as a nurse and enrolled at a local hospital. But as time moved on, other less happy memories started flooding back, clamouring for her attention, and as she began her training, she became increasingly disturbed by them.

Kieks (left) resting while training as a nurse after the war (1946)

As 1945 rolled on towards 1946, Kieks heard from Truida and Jan Boone that Kees had been interrogated by the police and would probably face trial at some time. The way that Willem, and now Kees, were being hounded by the authorities made her feel nervous. What would happen if her own story became known, and how would it be interpreted?

The memories of the wartime events were continuing to prey on her mind all the time now. The most deeply etched memory was her experience in the field when she had been briefly captured by the convoy guards, her slow, slow roll in the snow, rolling in full view of the guards, the guard silhouetted against the grey sky, approaching closer and closer, and then turning away. Lying there stock-still, for hour after hour, petrified that at any moment the soldier would come back and shoot. The cracking machine-gun fire, the piercing screams, the guns roaring long after the screams had stopped.

Sometimes she thought about the soldier who had started to walk towards her and then turned. Was he the man she had seduced? Had he seen a movement? Had he seen her there, recognised her and let her lie away from the other hostages, to escape the firing squad? Or had he just got up to relieve himself, and not seen further than a few inches beyond his boots?

As Kieks wondered if she should step forward and provide support for Kees, she became increasingly worried that the questioning would lead to her humiliating and painful story being revealed. Would the courts see her actions as having been a desperate effort to save her life, or would they turn round and accuse her of treason? That was the accusation being levelled at Kees. It was frightening that the people who had risked their lives fighting against the Germans, people like Willem and Kees, were being pursued by the police, while the people who had done nothing were encouraged to get on with rebuilding their lives.

She was to replay the events of that day in her mind many times: Was there anything else she could have done to escape with her life? The answer was always no. She had used the only means she had of saving her life. If she had gone back to Kees sooner, would their romance have continued? That she didn't know. Each time she replayed the events, they became more vivid, but there was never any closure. She couldn't possibly process the devastating memories, nor comprehend their full effect.

In 1947, when the diary of Anne Frank was published, Kieks was quick to get a copy. She could readily identify with the events and the atmosphere described in the house, the tensions and the fear, but reading it left her with a hollow sense of frustration.

For Kieks, it brought into focus many of the unsettling events following her own family's efforts. She dwelled despondently on the way they had been repaid for their years of struggle by a summons to an anti-Semitism tribunal. How could the complex ordeal be distilled into such a trivial accusation? She thought again of the ordeal that Kees was facing. Jan Boone and Truida were still passing on news about the likely trial, and Jan expected to be questioned as a witness. He was worried about how the investigators were focusing on the details of Kees's involvement with the SS at the start of the war, and ignoring how he had relentlessly fought for Holland against the Germans in the later years.

Kieks felt families such as hers were being ignored, the only recognition her family had received being the quiet words of kindness from the tribunal chairman at the end of Willem's hearing. She felt deeply hurt and forsaken. She clearly recognised the abysmally difficult conditions experienced by Anne Frank and those like her who had hidden in shelters, but in the years immediately after the war, she felt the diary and popular sentiment seemed to completely overlook the people who had chosen to protect them. In Anne Frank's case, that disregard had been an inevitable consequence of the circumstances, the Franks and the families who protected them had lived apart, and anyway, the journal had been written as a private journal, never intended to be published for the world to read. When she read the diary it also struck her that the events Anne Frank had experienced seemed so ordinary and mundane, sometimes quite similar to how their own everyday routines had been. Her own experiences made the security blunders these people had made jump out of the page at her. The Franks had not properly considered their own version of Willem's stern security strictures, but there again: they had not been able to go out in the street to learn what was needed to survive the Nazi Occupation.

The feelings of bitterness and acrimony that welled up when Kieks read the diary were intense. She knew her reaction was not quite rational but, these days, she couldn't quite control the overwhelming waves of anger that seemed to spring out of nowhere, pushing rational thought aside.

She kept coming back to the possibility of testifying in Kees's trial, and worrying that their probing questions might lead them to the story about the German guard in the field. That wouldn't just be publicly humiliating and dangerous for her and the family; the overriding fear was that she might be charged with treason.[42] She played the

---

[42] After the war, the Dutch people meted out their own punishment for collaborators and '*Moffenmeiden*' (women who had had 'relations' with the Nazis), who were rounded up and publicly humiliated by having their heads shaven and painted orange. Some were lynched or otherwise punished without trial; those who were known to have worked with the *Waffen SS* were used to clear minefields, suffering losses accordingly. Many were later sentenced by court for treason.

events over in her mind again and again, trying to recollect exactly what had happened, how she could describe it in a way that didn't bring shame to the family. What would she say? How would she describe it?

She eventually discussed things with Jan Boone, and came to realise the significance in his preoccupation with Kees's links with the SS. It dawned on her that Kees's involvement with the SS at the start of the war was something that Jan had witnessed, but she had not. Perhaps, after all, it was reasonable for her to avoid the trial.

As she replayed those events from the snow-covered field in her mind, the nightmares started: the field, the snow, the trailers, the soldier. The torment always ended with her lying in the ditch looking up, the menacing German soldier outlined against the grey sky. She would wake up, sometimes paralysed in a cold sweat, sometimes screaming with fear.

Kees's story was slightly more complex than the one he had told Kieks in November 1944. Kieks had found his involvement with the *Waffen SS* abhorrent; after the war, the authorities also found it so. He would eventually pay for his dalliance with an investigation and trial. The investigation started in July 1945, where every step of his path through the war was explored, probed, tested with witnesses, challenged, and prepared for a report to the court. As was customary in Holland, the trial itself was a short review of the evidence gathered in the investigation, and completed in just a few days. For Kees the whole experience was protracted and deeply distressing. The proceedings were inscribed on the court record, providing later historians with the opportunity to explore the events, but that was little comfort to Kees.

The evidence presented was that immediately after Germany had invaded Holland, Kees had contacted his school friend, Jan Boone, and another friend, telling them of his intention to get training in the *Waffen SS,* infiltrating them to gain insight into how best to fight them from within the Resistance. There had been adverts in the newspapers for training courses and he had gone to Munich in June 1940 to attend such a course. The evidence also stated that while he was there, he had taken every opportunity to persuade other Dutch people to leave the training course and go back to Holland, singing patriotic Dutch songs on the piano and disrupting events as much as possible. It stated that in October that year, he had refused to take an oath to Hitler, resulting in his being sent to prison back in Holland and from there to the Sachsenhausen concentration camp in Germany. He had arrived at the camp in March 1941, and after eighteen months had emerged in September 1942. Returning to Holland, he had first gone to Zeeland for ten months and then had renewed his contact with Jan Boone and had headed to The Hague, finding refuge with the Okmas at Citroenstraat.

After the Gestapo search of Citroenstraat, he had stayed in the area around The Hague until about May 1944, when he had travelled to Dordrecht. During this time he was working with Douwe in Hillegom. The move to Dordrecht had been in response to his Resistance group being betrayed by a traitor, Pieter Marsman. Once the traitor was identified, the man was killed and after that Kees had departed for Dordrecht.

Kees had arrived in Hillegom just before *Dolle Dinsdag*, and a few days before Kieks had. He had stayed only a couple of weeks before moving on to Haarlemmermeer to start a new Resistance group. He claimed not to have made any effort to hide his past links with the *Waffen SS,* and some of the team there would later remember the truth of these details after the war was over. While at Haarlemmermeer he had undertaken a large number of sabotage activities, including raids on administration offices, and distribution of food stamps.

He remembered the transporting of weapons and deliveries around the area. There had been several close calls. In September 1944 there had been two incidents on successive days, both outside the area where he was commander: in the first there had been a shoot-out with the Germans and a narrow escape when the three Resistance fighters had almost crashed their car, and the next day the men delivering the weapons had been surprised by *Landwachters* at a farm and had been shot. Kieks' memory of that time was probably a confabulation of the two events.

After the war, in July 1945, Kees was arrested on a charge of treason on the basis of having joined the SS. There was speculation that some people in the area may have wanted him out of the way. He had been hiding on a farm and was arrested after a letter he had sent had been passed on to the 'special investigations police', a special group of police investigating wartime events. This letter had included mention that he had called off his engagement to Kieks.

He was interrogated by the special police, released, and sent for trial in 1949. Jan Boone was one of many witnesses interviewed, and in February 1949 Kees went to trial, which in Holland at that time was more of a formal review of the evidence gathered in the interview process. Kees was acquitted in the Special Court in Middelburg at the request of the prosecutor. One of the arguments presented was that legally he could not be found guilty of joining the enemy because he had refused to take the oath of allegiance to Hitler. The training he had taken was advertised as 'training with no strings attached'. In addition to his acquittal, the court went beyond the remit of the proceedings and commended him for his work in the Resistance.

The investigation and trial angered Kees tremendously, with his anger directed at the so-called 'heroes of *Dolle Dinsdag*' who had joined his group in September 1944, but had been too afraid to get involved with the truly dangerous dirty work. The only 'courage' they had shown was to turn on him after the war. He would later acknowledge that his link with the *SS* had been reckless; at his trial his lawyer had pointed out that he had since paid a high price with his time in Sachsenhausen concentration camp.

A report of the time also revealed more details of the story about the young German Jew in his Resistance group, Kareltje. The evidence came from a Ge van Buuren[43]. Van Buuren said that Kareltje had told Kees he was going to contact him to get a weapon, and Kees had subsequently told Van Buuren not to give Kareltje the gun because he was too young. On the same day Van Buuren had turned him down, Kareltje must have lost his temper because he had gone out and hit a German soldier with a brick and stolen his gun. It was shortly after this that Kareltje had died in a gun fight.

As Willem tried to rebuild the harmony of family life, he came across the letter from Scotland that had come at the start of the war, and remembered that first pang of fear as he had worried how it might be preceived by the Gestapo. He now wrote back to Archie Scott, thanking him for his

---

[43] Pronunciation: Ge van Buuren = *Hay fun Byur-in* (*G* is a guttural *h*).

letter and affirming that the whole family was well after surviving the war.

Archie had been in an Air Defence battery in Glasgow during the war, and afterwards he was part of the occupying forces in Belgium. When he received their letter, he took some leave and travelled across to visit the Okmas.

Archie in Belgium

He made several visits there, and when Kieks had an occasional afternoon off from nursing training, the two of them would take the family's growing brood of children down to the local beach and let them play in the sand. Kieks found it difficult to understand him, but their attempts at speaking French and his efforts to communicate were humorous, forcing her to concentrate on the challenge of understanding what he was trying to communicate and to stop feeling sorry for herself. She found herself increasingly enjoying his company, and relaxing away from Citroenstraat, taking her mind off all the tumultuous memories.

Archie and Douwe in 1945 (Archie was 5 foot 10 or 175 cm tall)

Other members of the family were having children; her closest sister, Trijntje, had had her first son in

November 1944, whom they named Miente, followed by a second, Popke, in 1946, and twin girls, Martha and Truida, in 1947. Her second sister, Truida, had married Jan and had had two boys, Pieter (1946) and Dirk (1949). Life was moving on with a fresh start for all the family.

The relationship between Archie and Kieks blossomed, and they began to talk of getting married. Kieks' mother was not sure: Scotland was a long way away, and little snippets of Archie's behaviour hinted at a big cultural gap. Kieks was enjoying the romance, and the promise of moving to Scotland held an extra allure: the chance to get away from Holland and all the bad memories of the war that seemed to stare back at her everywhere she looked, haunting her and invading the very fabric of her dreams. If she went to Scotland, she might escape this haunting, flee this vendetta by the authorities that had already engulfed Willem and Kees and seemed to rage around her.

As she succumbed to the courtship, the lure continued to pull at her and in May 1948 they got married. Kieks set off with him for a new life in Scotland, trying to leave her wartime memories behind.

The wedding of Kieks and Archie (1948)

Kieks and Archie with Ruurd's children, Dirk and Ineke, in attendance

Wedding of Kieks and Archie Scott

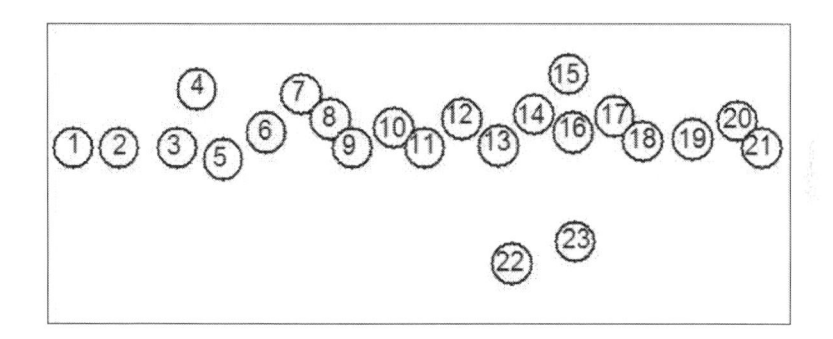

Wedding map

1) Tante Sibbel, sister of Kieks' Father; 2) Oom Jan Verdam, Sibbel's husband; 3) Martha; 4) Douwe; 5) Diny, wife of Willem; 6) Willem; 7) Jan Boone, husband of Truida; 8) Wil Spaans (with whom Kieks stayed at the end of the war); 9) Truida; 10) Ella; 11) Corrie, wife of Ruurd; 12) Tiny, wife of

239

Douwe; 13) Bessie Scott, sister of Archie; 14) Dirk, husband of Trijntje; 15) Ruurd; 16) Archie Scott; 17) Trijntje; 18) Kieks; 19) Moeder, Truida Okma; 20) Rev Muir Henderson, Church of Scotland minister in Rotterdam; 21) Alex McFarlane, Best Man; 22) Dirk, son of Ruurd; 23) Ineke, daughter of Ruurd

They travelled over to Glasgow and settled in the centre of the city. In 1953, their first son, Andrew (this author), was born, followed in 1956 by a second, David, and finally twin girls, Ella and Christine, in 1961. Kieks' mother occasionally visited Glasgow, and Kieks took the family over to Holland to visit the family every other summer for several years.

The early years in Scotland

The Scott family in Glasgow (from left): David, Kieks with Ella, Archie, Moeder, now Grandmother Okma ('Oma') with Christine, and Andrew

Andrew and David with Trijntje's husband, Dirk, on a family holiday on Texel, circa 1960

Even after the move to Glasgow and setting up a new life there, and despite all the pleasant distractions of raising a young family, the unresolved memories continued to haunt Kieks. Night after night she would wake up screaming, terrified, torn out of sleep by her recurring nightmare: slowly, slowly rolling in the snow and then looking up into the ominous profile of a German soldier silhouetted against the bleak grey sky, her moment of death at hand.

Some thirteen years after leaving Holland, just after the girls were born, Archie, at a loss as to how else to help her, persuaded her to seek psychiatric help, and he went with her on her first consultation.

With great effort, she started to recount her wartime experiences to the psychiatrist, in all their painful detail. He sat and listened quietly, occasionally asking probing questions as she spoke.

The war had finished some sixteen years previously, and the amazing stories of the exploits of the French Resistance had caught the public imagination, generating many fictional accounts, films and TV dramas in the intervening years. To those people who had never left Scotland, the exploits may have seemed just that:

dramatic fiction. No one will ever know what went through the psychiatrist's mind. It is quite possible he was a religious man, possibly with very clear Presbyterian views on what was right and what was wrong, as was common in Scotland at this time. It is quite possible that he had had little experience in dealing with foreign patients; Kieks' accent was quite strong and her English was not altogether fluent, especially when she became emotional. It is possible that he regarded post-traumatic stress as a man's disease, a soldier's disease. It is possible that he regarded compassion or empathy as unprofessional, a sin.

He pronounced his diagnosis. He said the stories were unbelievable, so unbelievable that they could only be a figment of her imagination. He twisted the knife further. If her story was true, it contained evidence that she was unfit to be a mother. The outrageous story of her lying in the snow with the German soldier was an indecent and shameful fabrication; if it was true, it proved she had no moral compass and was especially unfit to raise children. It implied she was morally incapable of bringing them up properly, and if that was the case, he had a responsibility to have the children removed and put into care. He would do this – unless she admitted to making up the whole story. What she really needed, he told her, was counselling to stop telling and believing these lies. His treatment would be to assist her to come to terms with reality, to curb her overactive imagination, and to realise that the events had never happened outside her head.

Whatever thoughts went through his mind, he could be confident that this diagnosis and its barbed codicil would ensure that this troublesome woman would never disturb the serenity of his consulting room again. He may well have regarded this as a quick, simple diagnosis, one of his more successful cases.

His reaction shocked Kieks to her core. She left incredulous and speechless with rage. As she returned home, his words came sharply into focus, for she knew he truly did have the power to have her children removed and put into foster care. I remember vividly, as a young child, her coming home that day with my father, cursing the psychiatrist and swearing she would never go back. The late afternoon light was fading, the lights on the Christmas tree were on, and my father's sister was babysitting us.

When she first came home, she was shouting and swearing, cursing the man roundly and repeatedly. In the days that followed, her raging emotions soon turned to fear and alarm, as the full significance of his cruel threat hit home; the possibility that we children might all be taken away. What menacing and callous new nightmare had this man visited upon her? This was only a decade after young women in Britain were being sent to mental institutions for the rest of their lives, for the mere act of having an illegitimate child. As a woman, she was powerless in the face of this cold propriety. The more she thought about this the more frightened she became, and she was adamant she would never have anything more to do with that man.

The threat from the Nazis was now in the past, but this new threat was very present. It would cast its shadow over her every day until all the children had left home. This greater fear of losing her children chilled her to the bone, overshadowing the nightmares that had haunted her since the war. She must now survive a new treachery, and bear the pain of salt rubbed viciously into her still-fresh wounds.

The words of the psychiatrist had far-reaching effects. My father did not know what to believe; he had heard many words of praise and support from her family in Holland, and allusions to her work in the Resistance, but he did not know the whole of my mother's story; she had only ever spoken of fragmented parts. Were these words of praise all based on lies? They both spoke separately to the church minister to find guidance. By the time Kieks spoke with him, the minister gave her some comfort, but seemed distant and detached. Sometime later, she went back to talk with him again but he was away on holiday, and instead she spoke with a church elder. He told her that 'they knew she made up these stories', but that they would still try to help her.

She was furious at this dismissal, and the way her confidence had been betrayed. It was absolutely clear to her that she could talk to no one, because no one would believe or respect what she had done. For the duration of the war she had felt that God had been looking over her, protecting her as she tried to do good. Now, she felt abandoned by Him, forsaken. She was proud of the brave things she had done, but now she was being forced to treat them as something to be ashamed of, as a vulgar secret to be smothered and hidden away. She never spoke to the minister or anyone from the church about her experiences again. Instead, she gave herself the focused goals of proving the psychiatrist wrong by bringing up her children as a virtuous and conscientious mother until they were old enough to leave home, and of trying to conform to the expectations of the alien society that surrounded her with its alien values.

A few years later, the teacher in my junior school asked us all to go and find out from our parents what they had done in the Second World War. We headed home with great excitement and a sense of competitiveness: Whose parents had had the most exciting story to tell?

As soon as I got home I asked my mother what she had done during the war. She was evasive at first, but eventually said, 'There were Jews in the fireplace'. The answer frightened me. A few weeks before, I had found a book in the back of the bookcase, hidden from view, containing upsetting pictures of Jews in concentration camps at the moment of liberation. Groups of skeletal bodies, piles of corpses and cremation ovens had stared out at me.

I hesitantly asked if she had been burning Jews, but she quickly corrected herself, 'No, no, the Jews were in a space *behind* the fireplace and the family had been hiding them'.

Now I sensed respectable excitement. 'Were you in the Resistance?' I asked.

'No, we have to say that there was no such thing as the Resistance,' she replied, her voice thick with stress. 'There were individuals who fought against the Germans, but we have to say there was no organisation'.

She couldn't put out of her mind the strictures of the psychiatrist, the threats that had prompted her to repeat the words of his formulaic admonishment. She quickly became very emotional, choked with tears and unable to say more.

I was confused. Later I heard from my father about his work in the anti-aircraft batteries near Glasgow, and decided to use his story to report to class. When we returned to school, we all agreed that the most exciting story was from one boy whose father had flown a Spitfire and had parachuted over England.

A while later I came across her small Dutch Bible, with most of the pages torn out and only a few fine paper leaves of the Gospels remaining. When I asked about it, she told me of the hunger during the *Hongerwinter* of the final year of the war, and how they had needed to smoke just to cope with the dreadful ache of the hunger. She exclaimed how painful it was for her to talk about these times, and quickly moved on to other things. The full extent of her story would elude me for many years.

As I look back to those times, I wonder if this psychiatrist's laziness and incompetence sowed the seeds that led to the eventual end of my parents' marriage. With this flawed diagnosis, my mother had been labelled a fanciful liar, and my father never knew how much to believe of what she said. The core of mutual respect that is needed to secure a marriage had been destroyed.

As time wore on, the nightmares became less frequent, suppressed and superseded by the threat of the psychiatrist's words, but they did not stop completely. I remember being asked occasionally if her screams had disturbed my childhood sleep.

Kieks did try to tell her story to the world in the late 1960s. The Reader's Digest was a popular magazine of the time that invited their readers to send in their stories. My mother had tried to write down her story, and she gave me the manuscript to read just before sending it off. Reading it, I found it incomprehensible, with many confusing allusions to parts of the story she couldn't tell. When I tried to ask her about it, she dismissed my questions angrily, exclaiming that some parts of her story could never be told. Her story was politely turned down by the magazine.

As we grew up in Glasgow, she seldom mentioned her experiences during the war, although occasionally glimpses slipped through. I decided to take up German, an option that would allow me to escape Latin, a subject I just couldn't come to terms with. At first she was angry at me for choosing to learn a language she detested, when I had never learnt her mother tongue. However, she quickly accepted my decision and was always willing to help me learn my vocabulary. She was briefly irritated by my choice of German but at least no one in the family was interested in psychiatry. That would have been completely unacceptable.

Perhaps we gained further insight from her reaction to a television programme that appeared in the 1970s. The programme was *''Allo 'Allo!'*, a comedy about the French Resistance. All the family enjoyed it – apart from my mother. It angered her, made her feel the Resistance was being laughed at, and she felt compelled to go out of the room whenever it was on.

Our family lived near Glasgow, and from 1963 we often travelled to the Isle of Eigg for summer holidays. The island is a small green patch among the Inner Hebrides, off the west of Scotland, about five miles from the mainland town of Mallaig. It is a few miles across, crowned by *An Sgùrr,* a dramatic towering block of granite almost 1,000 feet high at its centre, and swathed with attractive beaches on the west coast. Its population then was less than seventy and it was a wonderful wilderness of dramatic geology and beautiful beaches, including the 'Singing Sands', which screech noisily when people walk on them. At that time, there was a single farmhouse on the island that took guests, and those visitors who were prepared to put up with the absence of mains gas and the intermittent electricity would come for a week and explore the walks that range over the island. They were joined by occasional larger groups from schools or universities, who also camped or used a caravan nearby.

The Eigg landscape with the granite An Sgùrr forming the skyline

One summer, in about 1976, my mother travelled up with the family by train to Mallaig and on to Eigg, as she had done so often before. They went to stay with the family at Laig Farm, where Margaret Kirk, the proprietor, was now a good family friend. The large house now had running water and a generator that provided electricity in the evening, facilities that were still not available in many of the other houses on the island. On this occasion it was crowded, as a group of German school children were visiting for a few days. As Kieks strolled around, she caught sight of one of the teachers, and froze in shock: She was convinced she was staring at the face of the guard she had seduced all those years ago. A startled look, of recognition perhaps, passed across his face also, and an hour later she received a message from one of the guesthouse helpers. The teacher would like to meet with her privately, and would she please join him in one of the quieter communal rooms?

In blind horror she grabbed a coat and hastened out into the wild countryside. She walked for over an hour, and eventually came back to a barn on the edge of the farm. She sat there for several hours silently, filled with dread, unable to face going back into the building, and the possibility of having to speak to this man. Later, when it was dark, she heard people out on the farm calling for her and looking around with torches. She went back in, but carefully avoided all the common rooms and any possible meeting with any of the Germans.

Following the disruption caused by the search, the teacher perhaps understood something of her feelings and seemed to avoid her from then on. As was common with such groups, he and the German party left the next day on an expedition and would camp for a few nights. My father was bewildered at what had happened, uncomprehending as to why she had completely disappeared for four hours, and angry with embarrassment because of the search parties that had gone out to look for her. She would offer no word of explanation to him or anyone else.

Later, they each spoke to me separately on the phone: my father venting his frustration at her disappearance and my mother talking only of a man she had met during the war, someone she absolutely couldn't speak to now.

The family did wonder about this event on Eigg. When I spoke to the proprietor, Margaret Kirk, she was politely dubious and uncharacteristically reluctant to get involved in a discussion. Some thought that the experience of unexpectedly meeting German speakers may have triggered a false memory in my mother; the diagnosis of the psychiatrist still left its shadow. On the other hand, the shooting of civilians, as my mother later described, was a war crime. If the teacher was asked about my mother's reaction, he had a very strong motive to deny the story, even if it were true.

In October 1979, seventeen years after our mother had visited the psychiatrist, my sisters left home to go to university, the last of the children to leave home.

In December that year, just three months after the departure of the girls, the whole Okma family was part of a group of ninety-six people who were honoured by the Israeli government through their official memorial to victims of the Holocaust, *Yad Vashem*. The memorial recognised the role and sacrifices the family had made in sheltering Jews during the war, and awarded them the *Medal of the Righteous,* inscribed with the words *'Whosoever saves a single life, saves an entire universe' (Mishnah, Sanhedrin 4:5).* Their names were to be added to the Wall of Honour in Jerusalem's Garden of the Righteous.

The award was made only when Jews had nominated individuals and provided testimony to confirm that the nominees had saved their lives. More than thirty-four years after the war, the family was presented with the award in the Utrecht Congress Centre in Holland, an eventual acknowledgement of their role in saving the *onderduikers* from Nazi capture and certain death. *Yad Vashem* was mandated to pay tribute to those people who had 'acted in stark contrast to the mainstream of indifference and hostility that prevailed in the darkest time of history'.

The *Yad Vashem* records would show that the first letter on the Okma file was one from the Van Gelderens; clearly they were keen to record how much they fully appreciated the efforts that the Okmas had gone to in looking after them. The Hekshers and Kurt Lewin also provided testimony about the family's bravery and kindness in risking their lives to help them, with Kurt also highlighting how much Teun van Dien had done to save his life.

Sallie Hekscher and Chris Lewin were present, but Lien and Bram were absent, while the Van Gelderens had both died just before the award was publicly announced. Bram explained that he had to look after his two-year-old son. His son was the age that he had been when Kieks had played with little Jantje and made sure he was safely sheltered through the war.

Later there was a reception with the Dutch Ambassador at the Kelvingrove Art Gallery in Glasgow. Kieks was humbled and honoured to receive this acknowledgement. Though the ordeal had been so many years ago, her life had been inexorably affected by her experiences, and she wore the award, a small decorative pin, proudly on her lapel for many years to come.

YAD VASHEM
MARTYRS' AND HEROES'
REMEMBRANCE AUTHORITY
JERUSALEM

Jerusalem, November 30, 1979

Mrs. Grietje Scott-Okma
59, Stirling Ave
Westerton, Bearsden
Scotland
United Kingdom

Dear Madame,

I have the honour to inform you that the Commission for Designation of the Just of Yad Vashem decided after due deliberation to bestow upon you, your late mother, your brother, sister-in-law and sisters the Medal of the Righteous for the bravery and human kindness you showed in risking your lives in order to save Jews during the Holocaust.

The Medal will be presented to you by the Israeli Embassy in The Hague.

You will be notified of the exact date of the presentation of the Medal in the near future.

Please accept our best wishes and our gratitude.

Dr. Moshe Bejski
President of the Commission
for the Just

The letter announcing the award of the Yad Vashem Medal of the Righteous

In 1980, Kieks was persuaded by her nieces and sisters in Holland to apply for a Dutch Resistance pension. The memories of the guard approaching silhouetted against the sky, the screams and the gunfire in the field had at last started to fade, but at the same time she and Archie had separated and her financial circumstances in Glasgow were making life uncomfortable. She applied for a disability pension from a Dutch organisation called *Stichting 1940-1945*, an organisation funded to help former members of the wartime Resistance. As she put together her application for her Resistance pension, her sister, Trijntje, managed to make contact with Kees, who agreed to provide evidence in support of Kieks' application.

Kees was already receiving a pension, and provided testimony in the form of a short letter to the *Stichting 1940-1945*. As a recognised Resistance commander his statement was not challenged. His letter was short (see Annex 2), but it confirmed the outlines of her claims: that she had been with the Resistance, acting as a courier, taking part in operations, setting up links with other groups, taking part in sheltering *onderduikers*, and it linked her with other high-profile individuals also known to have been in the Resistance. Twenty years too late, it proved that what she had revealed to the psychiatrist was not a tissue of lies.

As she wrote her application for the pension, she was again forced to confront and describe her wartime experiences in detail. This released many memories that she had managed to keep bottled up for almost half a century. The terrifying nightmares of the 1960s returned; the vivid image of the German *Wehrmacht* guard standing over her, silhouetted against the grey sky, reminding her of a time when she alone, of perhaps twenty Dutch people, had escaped a firing squad and cheated death.

Some time later, she was interviewed by a Pensions official and recounted her story in a quiet room, describing the various events she had been caught up in; dramatic, sometimes intimate vignettes that were still as vivid as if they had happened yesterday. They were also scrambled, fragments tumbling forth out of order, with strange gaps where the continuity didn't seem to fit. As she talked, she felt a sense of heightened unreality in the peaceful interview room. At times she discerned an air of incredulity from the man, but at the same time she sensed compassion and reassurance in his responses. She was relieved that her story had already been corroborated by Kees, the man who 'had been there'. When she came out of the hearing she was utterly emotionally drained. At last she had been able to tell her story without criticism or rebuke, but the strain had been intense, exhausting to dredge through all that long-buried pain. She swore that if her application was turned down, she would never apply again, never relive the memories.

As she waited for the decision on her application, she was surprised to find how much the hearing had helped her cope with the memories. Having finally spoken them out loud, she could now handle them in a way she had not experienced before. The atmosphere of suspended disbelief seemed to make them less real and intrusive, while the compassion and the moral support eased her self-doubt and the feelings of shame and anger she had tried to fight for so many years.

She was awarded the pension. The sense of psychological support and respect, and the boost it gave to her self-esteem, was at least as valuable to her as the financial benefit. She also took comfort from the evidence that was now out there to support her story, the evidence filed with *Yad Vashem*, and the letter from Kees to the

Pensions tribunal – a final, open recognition and confirmation of the shrouded truth of her story. For the first time, the intense feelings of persecution and anger ebbed away and she was able to talk.

In 1986, Trijntje told her that Kees had been interviewed on Dutch TV and there were stories everywhere about his wartime exploits. They had been triggered by the film that was appearing all over Holland, *'De Aanslag'*, or 'The Assault'. It told the story of the police inspector's assassination in October 1944, and the fallout from that event. It was clear that it was the same incident as the one Kees had talked about before going off to Haarlem, and the film was to win an Oscar for the 'Best Foreign Language Film'. Trijntje and her daughters managed to get in touch with Kees again, and met him to reminisce over his time in Citroenstraat.

Even after my mother went through this final challenge and its successful outcome, there was another last twist in the narrative. My wife and I had our first son, Colin, in 1985, and in January 1987, I was diagnosed with Acute Myeloid Leukaemia, with my chance of surviving put at

50%. I now had my own struggle for survival – with a less dramatic backdrop than hers, but with the same stakes. As the family rallied round to support me, my mother's struggle and her final recognition were relegated to the margins for a while. My treatment was stressful but very successful, and after a bone marrow transplant from my brother, I returned to work in December that year. I was preoccupied with getting back to living a normal family life and to resuming responsibilities at work, and for a while my mother and I were somewhat distant and detached.

I received a temporary posting in 1992 to work at the US Naval Research Laboratory in Washington DC. My mother came to visit me in Washington, and on the first evening, the state of my health was an inevitable topic of conversation. The talk drifted into her trip to Holland for the hearing on her pension, several years before the diagnosis. She talked first about the pension interview, which led her, at long last, to talk to me about the details of the war, describing where the Jews had been hiding, how they had been brought to the house, how she had helped bring in food, and how the family had worked together to support the household during the war. The events were dramatic, but her account involved unfamiliar and confusing names, with haphazard meanderings from one story to another, and I was soon very confused.

When I went to bed, the fragments of stories flitted around my mind, and I lay there, trying to fit them together to form a more complete picture. I had difficulty getting to sleep, and after a while I found a scrap of paper, and wrote down some headings, simply to follow the sequence and spot the inconsistencies where one memory had entangled with another. This led to more questions arising, and over two weeks in 1992, as we walked round taking in the sights of Washington, and sat over meals in restaurants and my apartment, she talked of more memories; vivid vignettes of the various incidents she had been caught up in. The story was something far more dramatic and complex than any of us in the family had ever suspected.

I worked on capturing, assimilating and writing the story behind 'the Jews in the fireplace' for some two years, and then in 1994 showed it to friends and family. My mother's sister, Trijntje, and her family identified some inaccuracies, and after correcting them I sent out further copies and put the book to one side.

When she first started telling me the story, it still produced an overwhelming anger in her, and she couldn't bring herself to talk about many of the events now described in this book. She could talk of the struggles to feed the extra mouths, the early events before the war, and the arrival of the Jews, little excitements like Willem stealing the suckling pig, and taking Jantje to the potato fields. She talked of delivering newsletters at night, guiding soldiers with her white envelope, and going into houses to prepare food for British parachutists. She also spoke of the frequent nightmares of the firing squad, and although she was careful to avoid spelling out exactly what had happened between her and the guard, she described the manhandling of the trailer with the secret weapon, referring obliquely to using her own 'secret weapon' (a description that I did not understand for a long time), and stumbling around in the dark trying to avoid the bodies lying in that field. Sorting these fragments out, putting them into order and into context, finally expressing and processing them, helped to calm her down.

At first, she tried to hide some of the details: her relationship with Kees, then his link with the *Waffen SS* and her reaction to this, and the events in Leeuwarden which had caused her to be up in North Holland and led to the incident with the secret weapon. I could sense that the telling of the story provided a therapy, and my frequent challenges to clarify the confusions caused her to rethink what had happened, and when, and who actually had been responsible for what. The order of events was particularly confused, and I started putting a month and year to each small fragment of the story, striving to make sense of the whole story. In the process of answering my questions and recognising the admiration from the family, her temperament changed. Her anger and unpredictability, which had often been close to the surface, receded.

In 1996, I heard that Kurt (Chris) Lewin had written his own journal and shortly after, Trijntje received a bound copy, with the impression that it was about to be published.[44] My mother and Trijntje remembered how he had frequently locked himself in the family bathroom in Citroenstraat, and now it was apparent that he had been writing his diaries rather than the detective stories he had

---

[44] *'Dagboek in Oorlogstijd'* by Kurt Lewin, alias Christiaan Gans; foreword dated 17 February 1995, now available online.

claimed. In the Seventies, he had shown his notebooks to his daughter, Lisette, and she had persuaded him to write them up as a book, with an attempt to capture the exact atmosphere of the time.

The refugees had never been privy to any of the details of the Resistance, so although Kieks was identified as the family contact with the Resistance, the details were absent in his journal. However, life in the house was portrayed in detail. The Okma family had been given the name Oldersma, with fictitious names given to each of the family members, and he had painted a picture of life in the household as he had experienced it. He had paid for the printing of fifty copies, sending one to Trijntje as a courtesy and to help her understand how he had felt during that time.

The Okma family were not pleased by the book. During the war they had exposed their own human failings as they sought to protect and feed five Jews in their house for three years, and there had been frictions as two cultures had rubbed together, but they had saved the man's life and the lives of his fellow refugees. My mother scanned through it, and took pleasure in noting how completely unaware he had been of the role she and

Willem had played in the Resistance. She later tried to analyse his story, but often got distracted by angry thoughts and memories.

As he prepared his book, Chris had gone back to Citroenstraat with his daughter and revisited the secret chamber, taking photographs of the entrance and the interior, which was now stripped of the fittings and shelving that Willem had made for their wartime shelter. His photographs showed the entrance to the secret chamber, a small square hole, barely a shoulders' width across, highlighting quite how small the entrance was and how difficult it would have been to climb through quickly.

Chris Lewin and his daughter, Lisette, revisit Citroenstraat and the entrance to the secret chamber, in the 1980s or 1990s. Behind Chris, the door into the secret chamber can be seen.

Chris Lewin standing beside the entrance intio the secret room. The small size of the entrance is clear

Some years later, I exchanged messages with Chris's daughter, Lisette. She explained that her father's book had never been intended for publication and only a few copies had been printed and bound. Writing his memoir had helped Chris in the same way that the writing of this book has helped my mother. Lisette also mentioned another book that her father had been writing during the war. It had been an academic treatise on economics and he had been disappointed at how little interest there had been in the house when he had announced it was finished. I thought about this and wondered if my mother might have misconstrued words on academic research and economics and ended up with recollections of 'detective work' and 'making money'.

In about 1997, my mother gave my manuscript to her solicitor, who read it and told her he thought he might be able to get it published. He passed it on to a literary agent, but later my mother told me the agent had returned it. In 2010 I met the solicitor on another matter and we discussed the rejection. He was positive about the story and encouraged me to try again to get it published.

For decades my mother had thought that the family's efforts in sheltering the Jews had been ignored and neglected, and that the work of the Resistance had been dismissed as pointless and irrelevant. Now she finds that her wartime activities are touched on by several written accounts. There is the work of Chris, the account in this book of own memories, a separate unpublished set of diaries kept by Salomon Hecksher and more recently we discovered that Ernst van Gelderen, son of Joop, had written a fourth book, the story of his family's memories and travels, entitled *'I missed my train'*, which was intended for their children and grandchildren's posterity. The diary that Sallie had kept during the war was originally regarded as just a small journal that mainly described the festive events, such as birthday parties for the members of the Okma family. It was said to describe the delicious food and drink, which had been so plentiful in the first year, and the suckling pig which had cheered everyone up but which Sallie had declined to eat. In recent weeks it has been read more closely and provides yet more details of the atmosphere and events in the house.

Kieks had been surprised by how much publicity there had been for Kees's role in assassinating a police inspector: one single event, but the focus of an Oscar-winning film. The years had passed, and in some ways the memories had faded, but in the late 1990s, the memories came flooding back, as the mental barriers that once silenced her were removed. As I wrote in 2000, her memories were fading faster, but she had had recognition from the family and that had given her some closure and satisfaction.

When I was ten years old my mother had told me 'there were Jews behind the fireplace'. It hadn't made any sense then, and the hidden story had profoundly coloured the years between, but now I feel I understand.

Epilogue: 2012 – A 90th Birthday Party

With time, further fragments appeared, almost seventy years after they happened. The full story of the horrendous events that happened in Leeuwarden was not told until a few months before Kieks' 90th birthday. It filled a gap I had always known existed: Why had she gone to a town on the other side of the country from where she lived? I suspected these memories were more fragile and may have been distorted with time. Now the memories were fading quickly; when I asked her about some other events of the time, she could no longer remember the details. She said that she had forgotten the things that she told me, and she had to tell me a few last things she had tried to keep secret, because they were still going round in her head and annoying her.

In January 2012, the family arranged a party to celebrate Kieks' 90th birthday. I told part of the story to her local newspaper to commemorate the birthday, and was soon syndicated across Scotland. For the first time in her life, people she barely knew in her sheltered housing complex came up to her and congratulated her on what she had done during the war. In a quiet way, she was very pleased. Her response persuaded me to investigate getting this book published.

The story has had several working titles as it evolved. For a while it was called 'A roll in the snow', but this seemed trite, and later 'Silhouettes from the past', before I settled on the current one.

As I put the manuscript into its final form, Trijntje's son, Miente, identified another set of inaccuracies, and I have gratefully adopted his suggestions. It was only at a very late stage that I discovered the role and prominence that Kees had had in the Resistance at a national level. I had misread my mother's handwriting in a letter she had sent me with the translation of his letter of support, and so I had misspelt his surname, and as a result I had not been able to trace him on the Internet.

We can now be a little more open about what happened, as those who might be hurt are no longer here. Kieks is the last of her siblings; her remaining sister, Truida, and her husband, Jan Boone, died just a few years ago. With the death of my mothe in January 2016, only

Bram and Donald, Sallie's children; Chris's daughter, Lisette; and Ernst and Carrie, Joop's children, are still alive. I have exchanged emails with Bram, Lisette and Ernst, and appreciate their comments on the text.

In a concluding revelation to my mother's story in 2015, the family of the one remaining key character, Kees, got in contact with me. Dirk Jan Laman, whose mother-in-law was the daughter of Kees, contacted me and provided me with some of the background to Kees's own experience before and after he had been with Kieks. He too is writing a book. The last few pieces of the jigsaw have fallen into place.

Kieks died peacefully in her sleep on 4 January 2016.

Acknowledgements

I owe thanks to a number of people who have helped my write this book.

I am immensely grateful to my cousin, Miente, for his valuable comments and for checking and correcting some of the key facts connected with his father, Dirk, and his uncle, Sjoerd, and a number of other errors elsewhere. He has read the manuscript repeatedly and patiently, advising me on much of the history and events that were happening at the time. He also subsequently put me in touch with Lisette Lewin, which has led to an interesting dialogue.

I also wish to thank the children of the refugees, Bram Hekscher, Ernst van Gelderen and Lisette Lewin, who have all kindly provided me with further information about the events that their parents experienced during the war. Lisette, Bram and Ernst have patiently reviewed earlier versions of this manuscript, corrected the chronology and helped me develop what I hope is a more balanced description of life in the house and events after the war. Ernst kindly sent me an abstract of the book he had written for his children and grandchildren, and Lisette also thoughtfully sent me a number of notes relating to events. I have used these notes to edit the account in the book.

Thanks are due to the *Largs & Millport Weekly News* and the *Scottish Daily Record,* whose interest and recognition of my mother's activities persuaded me to make the final changes to get this electronically recorded and into print.

In May 2015, I received a letter from Dirk van Laman, the son-in-law of Kees's daughter. He had seen parts of the *Scottish Daily Record* when he had been tracing the Krijger family history, and he had sought to find Grietje Okma, whom Kees had written about. This opened a new perspective on what had happened, so long ago. He provided an account that told of Kees and Kieks being engaged for a while – something my mother had never mentioned – and revealed that Kees had been to trial in 1949. He also explained Kees's link with Jan Boone, and their friendship dating back to their school days. Understanding the relationship between Kees and Kieks was particularly important for me because my mother had mostly hidden the relationship from us, leaving me with an impression that she had perhaps been infatuated with him but that he had had less feelings for her. Kees's trial also put in context some other comments she had made about 'lots of people being tried for collaboration'. I thank Dirk and his mother-in-law for his valuable insights.

I am very grateful to Lisette for her permission to use photographs of the entrance and the interior of the secret chamber. I am also grateful to Pieter Vuljk who kindly provided photographs of the exterior of the house at Citroenstraat, and of the memorial at Haarlem, and to Dirk Jan Laman, who provided a photograph of Gommert Krijger (Kees).

I also wish to thank Nicky Beele, for her editing of this book, and providing some further background material that helps put it into the context of Dutch history.

I must also thank my brother, David, and my sisters, Ella and Christine, who also heard our mother's fragmented stories throughout their lives, and for their support in helping me to put this book together. They have told me that putting these stories together has given them a certain sense of peace and perspective on our upbringing.

Finally, I must thank my son, Colin, who made many valuable suggestions and critical sub-edits to help the flow of the book, and my wife, Linda, for her encouragement, advice and IT support.

Annex 1: Chronology of Events

Part 1

1938: Willem & Martha visit the Rhineland

1939: Willem & Martha visit Scotland; they return with Archie Scott who stays with the family for a few days

1939: Willem rents a house in Citroenstraat in The Hague. Douwe marries

1939 September 29th: War is declared between Germany and Britain, and WWII begins

1940 May: Germany invades Holland. Rotterdam city centre is destroyed by bombing and the Netherlands surrenders

1940 December: Secret room is completed

1942 September: Salomon (Piet) and Lien Hekscher arrive at the Okmas' door

1942 October: Joop and Bep van Gelderen brought to the Okmas by Piet Brakel

1942 November: Little Bram (Jantje) Hekscher is dropped off on the Okmas' doorstep

1943 July 15th: Kurt (Chris) Lewin avoids a raid and scrambles into the house via a roof window

1943 July 28th: Gommert (Kees) Krijger arrives

1943 October: The house is searched by the Gestapo

1944 January: Kieks gets engaged and starts courier work for the Resistance

1944 February: Willem & Diny, Trijntje & Dirk get married

1944 August: Kieks leaves Citroenstraat and goes to Douwe at Hillegom near Haarlem

1944 September 5th: *Dolle Dinsdag* – Mad Tuesday, when many Dutch people openly celebrate victory by the Allies and collaborators flee to Germany. Resistance workers forced to go into hiding afterwards

1944 September 17th: Allies parachute into Arnhem

1944 October 25th: Kees assassinates the police inspector

1944 November: Kieks discovers that Kees had been in the *Waffen SS*

1944 December: Kieks goes up to Leeuwarden; an attack by her cousin causes her to avoid a Gestapo trap

1945 January: Kieks is captured in the countryside, and escapes with 'a roll in the snow'

1945 May 5th: Germany surrenders and WWII ends

Part 2

1945 July: Willem is called to tribunal

1945 July: Kees is arrested on a treason charge

1948 May: Kieks and Archie get married and move to Scotland

1962: Kieks visits a psychiatrist

1976: Kieks sees the German guard, now a teacher, on the Isle of Eigg

1979: The Okma family is recognised by *Yad Vashem*

1987: Kieks receives a Dutch pension for her Resistance work

1992: Kieks first tells her family about what happened during the war

1997: Kieks gives manuscript to lawyer to investigate publication

2010: Kieks' lawyer discusses rejection of the manuscript with Andrew

2012 January: Kieks celebrates her 90th birthday, and a few details of her exploits are published by the local press

2015: Kees's family relates new information about Kees and Kieks' wartime engagement and Kees's post-war trial

Annex 2: A Letter from Kees

This letter was the declaration provided by Kees to support Kieks' application for a pension for her work in the Dutch Resistance.

Letter to Stichting 1940-45   6 Sept 1980
District Bureau Zuid-Holland
3014 GP Rotterdam
Westersingel 23   H/sk/797

Dear Sir or Madam

In reply to your letter, I am writing to confirm that Mrs Scott-Okma was a member of the Knokploeg[45] (KP, Resistance Unit) based in Haarlem-Haarlemmermeer and surrounding area. She personally played a large part in the formation of this unit because she initiated the contact between me and Bob Allink. We stayed in the Biesbosch after the KP in The Hague was betrayed, and after the Atrocity in North Holland.

---

[45] The Dutch Resistance 'National Assault Group', a group of about 750 members conducting sabotage operations and occasional assassinations in 1944.

The people involved were her brother Douwe, Ben van Nat and Gerard Lemmert, and also Cor van Stam and Hein van Staveren.

As a result of her efforts we set up a KP Resistance Unit, building on the foundations that had been put in place by "Yeung Vaumont" (Marinus Vaumont) who was killed at the police station in Heemstede. In addition there were some younger ones who joined this group in Haarlemmermeer.

Mrs Scott-Okma acted as a courier from the very start of spring 1944 until the end of 1944 as far as I can remember. She did everything to keep the group functioning. She was quartermaster for the group that guarded the springwells in the Ringdijk of the Haarlemermeer around the time of Dolle Dinsdag (6 Sept)[46] in the Binnendijk of the Haarlemmermeer occupied the dropping points. (*There were 'springputten' in the dykes. Germans had put explosives in those and if England had invaded the Dutch beaches, the Germans would blow up those wells and with that the dyke would have failed, leading to floooding of the entire Haarlemermeer. The risk was estimated to be high and the Resistance guarded them at a distance*) She was sent out on reconnaissance missions. She moved weapons and kept contact with many helpers whenever needed.

In this role she was involved in the preparation of a number of raids, such as the one on the Head Office of the Police in Hoofddorp when Karel van Boesnack and Hein van Staveren

---

[46] Dolle Dinsdag was on the 5th September.

were set free. She also was also in the raid on the munitions depot of Vogelenzang in Bennebroek.

Prior to that, she had distributed large bundles of illegal newspapers for her brother, taking them down to Dordrecht. She was involved in the helping of Jews. She personally placed a Jewish child in Biesbosch near Dordrecht.

I saw her take part in so many clandestine activities that there are too many for me to mention each and every event, taking into account that it was 36 years ago. She was extraordinarily active, very good at keeping secrets, thoroughly trustworthy, discreet and brave.

If you wish more details I will be pleased to give you any help you require. I am convinced and I know from my own experience that she was an effective underground worker to the extent that if you could capture in words what she did when she was in the Resistance, you would capture the essence of what the Resistance was all about.

Trusting that I have given you sufficient information.

Yours sincerely,

G Krijger (Kees)

Annex 3: Comments on the Books by the Refugees' Families

We first heard from Trijntje in 1995 that someone was writing a book of their own about the years in Citroenstraat. In 1996, Kieks received what she thought was a draft copy which had been given to Trijntje. The author, the refugee Chris Lewin, died that year, as did another of the refugees, Lien Hekscher.

The book describes Chris's life during the war, including the years of his hiding with the Okmas, but the period in hiding and relations with others in the house is only a small section of a larger story. His daughter, Lisette, told me the book had not been intended for publication but only distributed to a few family and friends. Nineteen years later, it does now appear to be available on the Internet.

In Kieks' opinion his book was fairly accurate in most details. She thought, from her quick reading, that it claimed to have been written during the war, but minor points she spotted suggested it may have been written later than this. For example, the original draft identified 1945 as the year of Trijntje's wedding, whereas in fact the event took place in 1944. Trijntje proofread it and corrected these points, and also insisted on one other change: Chris had consistently expressed strong opinions about one of the extended family, and she wanted this to be changed throughout.

During the war, Chris had been told by Willem not to keep a diary, to avoid incriminating anyone, and Kieks concluded that he had written it clandestinely during the times he had locked himself in the bathroom. Since the errors were specifically in the dates of events, it is possible that he had not written the actual dates on the notebooks he had used.

Chris used false names in his book, and when I came across this, I realised I would either have to ignore his work or link it to my own. Since Chris's book appeared to have been published, I felt that the two separate commentaries were probably of extra interest because of the different perspectives on the same events, and because it would be relatively simple for anyone to find the true identities; for example, by tracking the details of the tributary recognition as recorded by *Yad Vashem*.

I have linked the relevant false names used by Chris to the true family names, with a few of Chris's comments on them in his book.

Oldersma – Okma: Chris describes the family as religious, anti-German and determined to protect them as God would expect them to

Magda – Martha

Els – Ella: 'not the most moderate in the family'

Wieke – Trijntje: 'maternity nurse; competent, calm with a good sense of humour'

Hendrika – Truida

Imke – Kieks: 'flighty and inconsequential' – a description that delighted Kieks because it emphasised how little he knew of her activities in the Resistance

Henk – Willem

Chris's daughter was Lisette Lewin, a Dutch author who has published several books including a novel, *'Voor bijna alles bang geweest'* (*Having feared almost everything*, 1989), about a child growing up during the war and the aftermath. Part is based on her father's book, where the

Okma family resembles the 'Glastra' family. The book describes the relationship of the child with *Tante* Froukje, which was based on her own relationship with Aunty Martha, and covers the post-war years up to the mid-Sixties, and her life as a student in Amsterdam.

She also wrote a second book, *'Herfstreis naar Dantzig' (Autumn Journey to Danzig)*[47], published in 1997 after her father's death. It describes the life of her father Kurt (Chris) and the tensions between Chris and the other refugees, from when he first went into hiding until after the war, when the other refugees broke all contact with him.

Ernst van Gelderen wrote a book for his family, recounting his own escape from the Nazis, entitled *'I missed my train'*. He also covers the escape of his sister and the experiences of their parents in the Okma household. A colleague wrote a short summary in English, which has been published in a US publication, *The Baltimore Jewish Times*, and which he kindly provided to me.

---

[47]http://www.bol.com/nl/s/boeken/zoekresultaten/Ntt/Herfstreis+naar+Dantzig/search/true/searchType/qck/N/8299/sI/true/sA/300/sc/books_all/index.html

Salomon Heksher also kept a diary, which was thought to contain little apart from details of the meals and festivities in the house. In the days before this was first published, I received an initial transcrit in English, showing it contained a number of details of life in the house. This will be examined more carefully in the fullness of time, but they have not influenced this book at the time of going to press.

Annex 4: A Poem by Salomon (Piet)

In dit pand, (Citroenstraat 18), boven in de nok,
Zaten wij jaren, als kippen op stok.
Te Zuchten en te wachten op betere tijden,
Tot we in '45 verlost werden uit ons lijden.
Mevrouw Okma en haar kinderen, hielpen ons door veel narigheid,
Een familie die zich zeker van andere onderscheidt.
Als kleine dank voor't redden van ons leven,
Willen wij hen deze herinnering geven.
                Lien en Piet
                Bram.

In this house, (18 Lemon Street), at the top of the keep,
We sat for years, like chickens roosting.
To sigh and to wait for better times,
Until '45 when we were released from our suffering.
Mrs Okma and her children, helping us through much misery,
A family to be distinguished from others, certainly.
As small thanks for saving our lives,

We want to give them this reminder.

        Lien and Piet

        Bram.

The commemoration plaque in the Garden of Remembrance at Yad Vashem in Jerusalem

The view from Yad Vashem

Printed in Great Britain
by Amazon